ABOUT THE AUTHOR

Andrew Fraser was born in Gateshead, Tyneside, in 1969. He studied Politics and Economics, which qualified him for precisely nothing, but was a lot of fun. His journalistic career progressed from covering garden fetes and drive-by shootings at the *Stockport Express Advertiser*, to grabbing a front-row seat at the bear pit of British celebrity culture in the noughties at *OK!* magazine, where he became Chief Writer. What he doesn't know about Kerry Katona, frankly, isn't worth knowing. Come to think of it, what he does know about Kerry Katona isn't worth knowing either. As well as Kerry, Katie Price, Peter Andre and the late Jade Goody, Andrew was lucky enough to interview the likes of Amy Winehouse, Chaka Khan, Lionel Richie, Joan and Jackie Collins, Linda Gray, 'Gazza' and Lindsay Lohan, to name but a few. His interview with Amy was featured in the recent biopic of her life. He moved to *Attitude* as Deputy Editor and Travel Editor for two years before leaving to pursue his dream of writing books. During his time there he charmed and chatted to, among others, Cher, Kylie, Boy George and ABBA's reclusive Agnetha Fältskog, a p

TRIPPING THE FLIGHT FANTASTIC

ADVENTURES IN SEARCH OF THE WORLD'S CHEAPEST AIRFARE

by

ANDREW FRASER

Bradt

First published in the UK in June 2016 by

Bradt Travel Guides Ltd
IDC House, The Vale, Chalfont St Peter, Bucks SL9 9RZ, England
www.bradtguides.com

Print version published in the USA by The Globe Pequot Press Inc,
PO Box 480, Guilford, Connecticut 06437-0480

Text copyright © 2016 Andrew Fraser
Edited by Jennifer Barclay
Fact-checking and proofreading Ian Smith and Janet Mears
Designed and typeset from the author's files by Pepi Bluck
Cover design and illustration by Robert Smith
Back cover design adapted by Pepi Bluck
Production managed by Sue Cooper, Bradt & Jellyfish Print Solutions

ISBN: 978 1 78477 039 6 (print)
e-ISBN: 978 1 78477 196 6 (e-pub)
e-ISBN: 978 1 78477 297 0 (mobi)

British Library Cataloguing in Publication Data
A catalogue record for this book is available from the British Library

Printed in the UK
Digital conversion by www.dataworks.co.in

CONTENTS

For my Mam and Dad.
Believe it or not, but I miss you. You were both amazing, in your *own* way. Which let's face it, is the best way to be amazing.

For my sister and brother, Chris and Neil,
because if I had been allowed to choose a sister and brother... well, c'mon, how could I have done better than this.

For Katie...
I don't need to write why, she will know why! Haha! What a superstar!

For my new Russian-German friend Phillip.
This book would not exist without you

And for Georgia,
I love you.

'BIZARRE TRAVEL PLANS ARE DANCING LESSONS FROM GOD'

Kurt Vonnegut

CHAPTER 1

LIFE (& TRAVEL) IS A BOWL OF CHERRIES

Since I was a kid, I always had a peculiar fondness for two things; bargains and the obscure. Sometimes, even now, they coalesce in the supermarket bargain bin. I've found some of the most amazing things there: strange soups, confused condiments and exotic ingredients which never caught on. I feel blessed to have them all to myself and I treasure their uniqueness while relating to them entirely and feeling their pain. Usually these products are just too classy, clever or ahead of their time to catch on. Think: the umbrella hat!

I first properly holidayed alone in 1991. This was a post-redundancy treat. I'd been paid to leave one of the worst jobs ever, insuring lifts and cranes for a now defunct company called National Vulcan in Manchester. I spent two miserable years there pretending to know what I was doing when I secretly didn't have a clue. I met one of my best friends in life, Katie, by the filing cabinets. 'I've been here for six months and I don't know what I'm meant to be doing,' I whispered. 'Shit. Neither do I,' she replied. 'I think it's something to do with lifts and cranes.' So we went and got drunk after work instead. We would hide our post because we didn't understand what it meant and we were scared to ask. On our last day we smuggled it out and threw it in the River Irwell. Relax, it was biodegradable. For this I earned the stately fee of £6,000 per annum. Yes, it was still appalling money back then, but given that I never actually *did* anything, it was probably a decent deal. I did, however, get £3,000 for leaving, which frankly was a result – and I was desperate to set off around the cities I had dreamed of visiting as a child.

I remember the European map half slathered in Soviet red – indicating that I probably would never be allowed to go to that area in my lifetime. Cities like Sofia, Krakow and Odessa, barely etched-in former nations like Lithuania, Armenia, Croatia... Just their names were so beautiful, melancholy, twinkly and magical. I had to go. I like to get what I'm told I can't have. And, with perfect timing, in 1989 the Berlin Wall had just come down. So off I went with my mate on a trip around Prague, Bratislava, Budapest and Vienna. Ironically, the flight I am going to find you now is almost certainly a lot cheaper than the ones I paid for back then. But emerging into Prague just a few months after the fall of communism was like being bathed in pure sunlight and oxygen. The city was thigh-tremblingly gorgeous, the people totally lacking in either Western charm or first-world cynicism.

Me and my mate Steve Jackson shared an entire nightclub with only a fey Czech ballet dancer pirouetting to *Bohemian Rhapsody*. The beer seemed expensive if it cost more than 30p a pint. We dined in the city's most beautiful and elaborately gilded former Communist Party restaurants alongside European aristocrats, who looked mortified to have to share their space with two oiks in shorts and baseball caps, and we devoured grand piles of meat with cabbage and dumplings, usually adorned with sour squirty cream and a cherry on the top. It cost pennies.

It was an amazing time. We spent one strange evening in a Slovakian country-and-western bar where locals, complete with ten-gallon hats, jodhpurs and cowboy boots, wailed 'Stand by your man' in the local language. My wisdom tooth had come up and I spent the first half of the night grinning like a maniac and clinging to my bed after taking 2p Slovakian painkillers. Budapest was similarly gorgeous, crazy and cheap and we ate the best black cherry ice cream ever for tuppence on Lake Balaton and rode four-wheel bikes around Margaret Island in the Danube. When we finished in Vienna, a giant wedding cake of a city, it seemed a little staid after our previous stops and prices were about six times higher. But I thought to myself, every holiday should be like this – an obscure bargain, ridiculous and inspiring. It's what I've sought ever since.

So when I look for a holiday I am prepared to go anywhere. Like my bargain bin delicacies, I just want it to be cheap, stimulating and maybe a bit of a 'find'. This may explain why I went where I went first…

So let's go back to the essence of this book. Or of the subtitle more like. I never did book that £1.48 flight. And yes, it *was* £1.48, (or $2.13, or perhaps… if you prefer €1.88… or maybe even 50.77 Czech Koruna… anyways, this is gonna get irritating hopping between currencies…so for the most part, we are just going to stick to good old

British pounds from here on... apologies. But let's pur-lease keep it like this for the sake of me and the Queen. We are both knocking on a bit, so I'm afraid we are leaving this to the rest of you guys to go on currencyconverter.com). Anyway, I found it. I had it in the palm of my hands; I was one credit-card click away from it. And I nearly booked it. But I didn't. I would have been buying it to prove a point. You see, I had no intention whatsoever of catching that flight. I would have been booking it for the sake of this book. Ultimately that didn't sit well with me, like buying food to throw away – somebody else could have benefited from that stupidly cheap air fare.

But there it is. Now you know it exists.

And I'm here to share with you a few of my adventures, which I hope will inspire you, and to show you how to get some ridiculously cheap flights for yourself; to help you dig out the flights which cost less than your latte en route to the airport. The cheapest flight I actually purchased was a whopping £3.30 – I know, exorbitant. There are mountains of flights for £1.48 or less out there, twinkling like stars in cyberspace, waiting for you to reach out and grab them and own them. The airlines don't appear keen to talk about them, but I'm here to show you how to harvest them like precious Galway oysters.

In researching this book, I flew to ten European cities and home in one month for £144 (or $210). It's a tough job, like being the Queen's personal food taster, but I want you to know that I did it all for you, honey. There were thrills, spills and bellyaches along the way. This isn't just for backpackers or cheapskates – although I hope there's something in here for them too. I prefer life's delicacies, and the money I saved was spent on beautiful hotels and gorgeous meals.

You know what they say: never go back. Thanks to a canny internet travel trick, which I will reveal to you later, I found out how to find the 'hidden' flights that cost next to nowt. 'Wahay!' I thought, until I tried to book a return. The cost was always massively higher than the original deal. 'Hmmm,' I thought; but what if you instead fly in a triangle A to B to C to A?

Boom! A Pandora's box of cheap travel unveiled itself. To make my point, and because I love adventures, I flew in a hendecagon. Now I didn't previously think that was a thing, let alone a possibility. That's A to B to C to D to E to F to G to H to I to J to K and back again to A. Phew! Maybe you can do better than that. I'll show you how.

Tripping means ditching the old A to B to A travel dictum and taking a more scenic route. Return flights are out. For example, my friend is flying home to Norway and then coming back to London. She has a week to spare, and she normally pays well over £120 for her return flights. I took a look and found her a new route. This time she will fly first to lovely, weird, occasionally beautiful, historic and fascinating Warsaw, where she will hang out for a few days.

Then she will fly on to Oslo for four nights at home, and back to London. This time the flights cost her £35. I'm not kidding. The money she saves will buy her and her boyfriend a decent little apartment in the centre of Warsaw for a few nights. And the cost of living there? A beer is 75 per cent cheaper in Warsaw than in London. A restaurant meal 70 per cent cheaper than in Edinburgh. It's a total win-win situation.

Oh and did I tell you? The flight to Oslo from Warsaw cost her just over £4.

Thanks to the internet, almost all airlines act like low-cost carriers these days; they just aren't so keen on letting you know about it. That's where I come in.

Tripping aims to do for air travel what the Slow Food movement did for eating. I'll be frank, if your travel diary means you just *have* to be in Marbella for one week in August, or the Hamptons are crying out for you each June – this maybe isn't for you. If it's every summer in Provence or Spring Break in Cancun, I'm not sure I have too much to offer you either.

For the rest of you, read on... because those aforementioned eejits are paying for us to go away on a shoestring. I mean, £3.30 ain't going to cover the stewardesses' heavy blue eyeshadow. But the airlines are making big bucks, so some of my fellow travellers were clearly paying for it. Just make sure it isn't you.

My first rule with everything is, if possible – never, ever pay full price for ANYTHING. Have you seen how much food the supermarkets and grocery stores throw away? It's a disgrace. That's why we should all be rifling through the bargain bins. With air travel, and here's the rub, no matter what the airlines try to convince you of, there is no such thing as full price, just people who pay more and people who pay less. The airlines will try and get as much as they can for a ticket, and if they have a half-empty flight heading across the skies of the world, the chances are they will keep reducing, reducing, reducing until the flight is fully sold out. Obviously there is not some sweet old lady in Doncaster, looking at her computer and shouting, 'Eric, Strasbourg's not selling. Shall we knock a tenner off it?' There are complicated computer algorithms that do this across the vast number of flights around the globe. The chances are they won't be reducing flight prices the night before you intend to travel – and they're unlikely to be considering that six months in advance. I'll help you know when as well as where to find them.

Finding the cheapest flights and creating your dream holiday itinerary is not an exact science. There's more than one way to do it. And there is more than one way to mess up and end up spending far more cash than you planned; so listen carefully and before you take off, you will be a dab hand at this. My tip is that you play with the system for a while. Create a few imaginary or dream itineraries and get practical at finding the right deals. Following my method will save you a packet and take you to places you never dreamed of. Sure, London, Paris, Rio, New York, Sydney and Tokyo are incredible world cities. And my method can take you there too. But are they the best the world has to offer? No. They're just the most obvious. And expensive. And overcrowded.

Shed your preconceptions. Join me on my adventure while you build your own. Let's go to magical cities, beaches and forests you've never heard of. It will be the dream holiday you never dreamed of. Let's find the food that the foodies are yet to discover. Let's find the places the guidebooks don't know about yet and splice it with some big hitters to create an itinerary which is unique and entirely yours, whether you have a week or three months to spare. And let's do it for a pittance.

HARVESTING OYSTERS

I've been aware for several years now that there are some stupidly cheap flights hanging around cyberspace – but I just didn't know where to find them. Sure, there were search engines out there, and you could find one-way flights for £40 or £50. Some of the better airline websites would show you which day in a particular month was cheapest to fly to a particular city. But it still seemed like a lot of to-ing and fro-ing, searching for information which surely someone must have collated into something tangible somewhere.

I knew there were loads of flights going for under a tenner, but how to find them easily and quickly? So I looked and searched and looked some more. Then one day last year, in a quiet moment, I grabbed my budget smartphone and tried again. It was all about asking the right question, and I hadn't known what it was until then. I Googled something along the lines of, 'Is there a search engine which allows me to put my destination as "anywhere"?' Instead of traipsing between sites looking for the cheapest flights from say, London to Lisbon – baffled by why we need so many search engines to do the same thing – and coming up with virtually the same results, I wanted the site to just tell me what my cheapest flight out of town next Tuesday would be, if I was prepared to go anywhere. Because surely anywhere can be fun, if you go with the right attitude, an open mind and a willing heart.

And up popped the answer. [Drum roll!] Skyscanner: an incredible resource for travellers which does not even appear to make a fuss of marketing its fundamental genius. Go figure! This was the first step towards getting what I had been searching for, my eureka moment.

So I dived right in and I searched for the cheapest flight out of London two weeks on Wednesday, and this is what I got: flights under £20 to twenty countries.

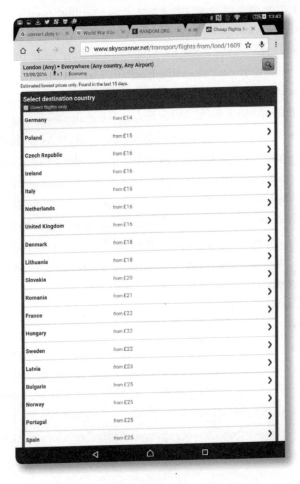

Splash out a couple more quid and you had Morocco at £22, Estonia or Montenegro for £23 and Macedonia for £25. And there was more than that. France and Germany had a dozen cities each for under £20. There were literally scores of flights across Europe for less than the cost of a meal for two in Pizza Express. Suddenly the world had become a great big bowl of cherries.

And before you protest, these weren't awful flights either. Luton to Copenhagen was £10 whether you left at 8.35 a.m. or 5.05 p.m.

That's when I hit the skids, though; a return flight from the Danish capital three or four days after my departure leapt up to £107. I found the same with Skopje, the Macedonian capital: a tenner to fly out – and around £100 to come back. Who knows what the logic behind this is? Perhaps the airlines realise that they can captivate us with a cheap outward bound flight, a headline grabber if you like. When you go to book the return and realise it is ten times more expensive, you shrug your shoulders and reckon you still got a bargain.

But there was another way. What if I just kept going forward, getting the cheap outward-bound flights? The only way is one-way! Fly in a circle, a triangle, or zig zag around. There are myriad three or four or five point routes back to your home city, more than a human brain can actually calculate. But how to find them? And how to find the cheapest and most interesting? It still meant a lot of to-ing and fro-ing on Skyscanner. I found cheap flights out of Copenhagen to Lithuania's beautiful Kaunas – but could I find my way from Kaunas to London? Which days? How much? Was there a better or cheaper route? Questions, questions!

And so that's when I made my second travel revelation: Skypicker now rebranded as Kiwi.com. Oh my goodness, Kiwi.com!

A Czech website, Kiwi.com hopped on the genius of Skyscanner, but realised that by arranging its data differently it could provide something even more invaluable.

Its first tweak was to dig out results which may include one or two changes en route (within a maximum journey time of around 50 hours).

The cost of flying from London to Rio, for example, could be cut by a third by changing in Madrid. It even allows for you to stay overnight. But... pfft! Who in their right mind would spend a single night in Madrid, the world's most fabulous, fun and easily charming capital city? In all of my research, connecting flights tended to be as cheap, or even cheaper, if you stopped off for a few days at your stepping stone city.

The trick is not to see the 'connecting' flight to Oslo or Madrid as a connecting flight or inconvenience at all, but as part of the experience and the holiday, an adventure which will save you a fortune.

Kiwi.com and Skyscanner will even allow you to search for the cheapest flight to a particular country over a broad swathe of dates. That means you don't need to specify where you fly in to. Suddenly, the cheapest flight I could find to the States, to NYC for £300, dropped to £149 by flying to Oslo and then Fort Lauderdale. For £551 I found this incredible transatlantic three week adventure: London. Oslo. Fort Lauderdale. Bogota. Cali. Medellin. Cartagena. Fort Lauderdale. London. The world had become a chocolate box – but which delicious nugget was I to consume first? Hmm...

So, while researching my trip, I'd looked at pretty much every itinerary possible. Obviously, the first stop needed to be special.

I had explored flights to Corsica via Strasbourg, an Italian adventure visiting several of its less celebrated cities via Brussels, Oslo to Poland was stupidly cheap – every time I thought I had reached my apex of excitement I found another option to tantalise my travel buds.

The USA and South America were definitely contenders but I thought it best to stay local. The wonder of Europe is that a 45-minute flight can transport you into a completely different world and culture. Come to think of it, you get that in the UK just travelling from Glasgow to Edinburgh. It's this piquancy of local flavour which gives the continent its tang.

I booked the first leg of my adventure 15 days before I was due to fly – a tad late I think now. As a pretty decent rule of thumb – last-minute booking does not work, ever. Equally, booking months in advance will not get you the best prices. Most airline computers are carefully watching price trends and ticket sales a few weeks before takeoff, hiking up prices and slashing them to the bone. For the really cheap flights, I'd recommend making your first booking 18 days before flying, if it's around Europe.

In my experience, the cheapest time to book varies from region to region, and there are more details on page 101. But remember, you're not just booking your first flight. You need to look at where you're going to head after that, too. Beautiful Deauville in Normandy was a snip at just over a fiver with Ryanair – but you can only really fly back from whence you came.

So I wasn't just looking at my next destination, I was looking at the hotspot after that. My priorities were:

1. Cheap as margarine
2. Thrilling and unknown – or at least leading to somewhere like that
3. Decent flight times
4. Good cheap connections to other cities which are all of the above

By the time it came to booking, I had already pretty much favourited a route through Vilnius, Lithuania and on to Kiev, Lviv and Odessa. It seemed to me to be the perfect time to visit this beautiful, beleaguered corner of Europe. After that, I was looking at sweeping down through Athens to Rome, Marseille, Lisbon and then home. The total journey price was coming in at just over £250, which was more than a trip like this needs to be – but what a trip! Europe, we are being told, is in crisis and all these cities seemed to be on the front line of economic, migrant and political turmoil, with unfriendly neighbours stirring the pot.

So I logged on to the search engines in early September when I was due to book my first flight. It was a thoroughly rotten day, England at its worst – wind whipping across London, a sea of grey forever and ever. The weather seemed to be taunting me. Summer Is Over. Oh crikey!

And I scrolled through the list of cities; scores of destinations, most of them alluring in their own special way. But one city just kept looking at me, winking at me I swear from amongst the legions of choices – at just over £10 from London Luton. Every time I contemplated the prospect of going there, I found a broad smile on my face. It was like the puppy in the pet shop with all the charm. It ticked every one of my boxes, tickled each of my proverbial fancies.

Suddenly there seemed to be no dilemma at all. I just couldn't look past it. It was too damn perfect, cheap, unexplored and more than a teeny bit weird. Googling the cityscape, it looked insane. And on top of all of this, Skopje, capital city of the Republic of Macedonia, has pretty much non-stop sunshine all the way through October. The last point which made it perfectly perfect was that I could see, by searching for flights out of town a few days later, there were heaps of interesting and low-cost options to the likes of Friedrichshafen in Bavaria, Barcelona, Venice, Sandefjord in Norway, Malmö and Milan. My mind was made up. My heart belonged to Skopje. And you don't hear that sentence every day.

CHAPTER 2
FROM THE BAZAAR TO THE RIDICULOUS

So, I'm in my taxi on the way out for a meal in the Old Town. And my driver asks, as everyone does in Skopje, 'What do you think of my city?'

'It's amazing,' I tell him, knowing this is nowhere near adequate. 'And interesting,' I add.

'Ah, yeah, interesting! Verrry, verrrrrrry interesting!' He smiles wryly.

We both laugh.

'Well,' he shrugs. 'This is the Balkans!'

'Maybe a bit too interesting for its own good,' I posit.

'There have been too many wars recently... around these parts. But not Macedonia. I hope never Macedonia,' he says. Then we both look pensive.

'I hope so too,' I tell him.

The next day I'm in a café-bar on the New Town side of the river drinking something weird which tastes vaguely of sex while assorted Macedonian bar and kitchen staff yell at each other. I think it's just how they communicate round these parts. It's a bit like north Manchester in that sense, but thankfully not any other. I've ordered the seafood salad and I'm panicking a bit because I've just remembered that this is one of Europe's most landlocked countries. Duh. I walked in, dazed from Skopje's mind-boggling cityscape, and the shouting bamboozled me even more. I panicked at the sight of the waitress with a large colony of hairy moles gathered above her top lip and a veneer of charm so thin a butterfly could brush against its shell and break it. And I start to laugh at it all. I'm in Skopje, surely Europe's most extraordinary, insane, funny, terrifying, weird, eccentric and yes, interesting capital city. This place has blown my mind and I love it and urge you to visit for reasons I will attempt to expand upon. It sure puts the trip back into trip. By the way, my salad has just arrived and I take everything back, it looks and tastes just fine. And it's very, very cheap. Even the expensive things are cheap in Skopje.

Maybe it's the giant luminous Alexander the Great with the flashing eyes, whose thrusting column turns from pink to cyan to mauve to puce. Maybe it's the giant gaping horse's arse statue which faces me from my hotel restaurant patio, or maybe it's the fact that Skopje's ancient Roman citadels, Baroque and Neoclassical monuments all look as good as new. They ought to. They were finished two weeks last Thursday... Some commentators have labelled Skopje kitsch. Or even, heaven forbid, camp. Skopje shrugs, pouts a little and replies, 'Camp – *moi*?' It's certainly divided the locals in the no longer obscure Macedonian capital. Personally, I bloody love it. I actually think it's beautiful. So shoot me.

Skopje is basically every single 1960s Charlton Heston film turned into bricks and mortar. Controversial ain't the word. From the minute I pull into the city centre I am transfixed. There is literally nowhere even approximately like this in the world. How much more adventure could you possibly get for the cost of a cheap takeaway pizza? God knows how many statues of national heroes there are in Skopje. I'm not sure anybody has lived long enough to count them all. It's frankly incredible that a country of some two million people should have so many great men (the women, Mother Teresa aside, are a bit thinner on the ground, it has to be said). If we had this many statues to British heroes, I think eventually we would run out of true heroes and have to start building statues to people who were just 'quite good' and then 'alright I suppose'. The newsreader Moira Stewart would have a plinth in a very crowded Trafalgar Square, as would Noddy Holder from Slade and the geezer who played Minty in *EastEnders* – Cliff Parisi, that was his name. There he would stand, thumbs proudly aloft outside the National Theatre. It's a project that has provoked mixed reactions from locals and foreigners alike. 'Oh my Gowd eet's so embarrasseeng,' said my London-based Macedonian friend Georgi in the best comedy east European accent ever. But others I spoke to out and about on the streets had a genuine pride in a city which is being entirely reimagined. 'Just look at all the tourists who come to see this now,' said one barman brimming with delight. 'They would never have come to Macedonia before. I don't care what the snobbish people say, it puts a smile on people's faces. I love our musical Alexander the Great.'

The giant Alex commands the centre of the once empty Macedonia Square. Kids run through the fountains and visitors stare agog when it comes into its own as night falls, like a giant musical box playing plinky plonky classical numbers while lions light up and fountains dance to the music. Not everyone is such a fan of it. Miroslav Grcev, professor of urban design at the University of Skopje, fumes, 'This is a crime against public space, culture, urbanism and art.' Bear in mind, this man created the not-exactly understated or shy and retiring Macedonian flag (a vision in yellow and orangey-red, which basically looks like the Union Jack, if you'd just dropped an acid tab) when the republic left Yugoslavia. People in glass houses, Miroslav...

'I stopped going to the centre of the city,' he sobbed. 'When I have to go past those monstrous, criminal colonnades and things which are not sculpture, I walk with my head down and my eyes to my shoes – the walk of a dead man.' Blimey, don't mince your words, mate.

It all reminds me of a similar hoo-hah in my home town of Gateshead when the council stuck a giant frog outside Barclays Bank on the High Street, presumably in a forlorn attempt to cheer things up a bit. The difference was that the Gateshead frog cost about £2.70 and a bag of chips. The Skopje 2014 project cost between 200 and 500 million euros, depending on who you believe, government or opposition. But its supporters argue there are imperative political reasons why Skopje needed its fantastical building spurt.

I had spent the previous day wandering, wondering and puzzling in the Old Bazaar, the largest Ottoman bazaar left standing in Europe – over a hundred years since they left this neck of the woods – which was just adjacent to my digs, the beautiful Stone Bridge Hotel, Turkish owned and decorated in opulent Ottoman style. They're not big on understatement in the Balkans, and I tend to agree, if you're gonna go for it, then really go for it. The Old Town is the longest-standing part of Skopje. Most of the rest was wiped out by a massive earthquake, which killed thousands back in 1963. Skopje lies at the edge of a geographical tectonic plate which is crunching into Europe like a particularly troublesome wisdom tooth. It also stands on the edge of a huge geopolitical fault line between East and West, Ottoman and Hapsburg, Muslim and Christian.

The River Vardar very much cuts the city into two separate worlds. While the new city gleams like a pristine utopia, this part of town is a bit crumbling and ramshackle by comparison, but none the worse for it. Both have their merits but it's hard to see them as part of the same whole. That's just one of the challenges facing Macedonia right now.

In the bazaar, with its countless minarets, old ladies in burkhas sell you delicious, home-made baklava soaked in honey and there are mosques, barber shops and many shisha bars. You can practically smell the sultan's slippers as he would have been carried through here in a gilded carriage. The young men I see around me have beards which aren't exactly of the hipster variety. As Muslims, they would have been valued and respected citizens of the Ottoman Empire. Not like those Slav Macedonians, or whatever they like to call themselves these days, living across the river. Not to mention the Greeks, Bulgars, Jews, Serbs, Armenians and whoever else was crowding the neighbourhood.

This bazaar is certainly no sanitised tourist trap. It's home to a big Albanian and Roma population. The town of Suto Orizari, just down the road, has Europe's only Roma mayor. As I stop to fill up on thick Turkish coffee, the call of the muezzin from Skopje's many mosques and minarets seems to slither through the city, wrap itself around the bazaar's crumbling walls and soak into my consciousness. It's a haunting sound and I no longer feel that I am in a crazy east European citadel, but deep in the heart of the Middle East.

In early twentieth-century Macedonia, people lived together cheek by jowl. Nobody predominated. But one by one the different races and nations mostly fled and were replaced by people from other parts of the Ottoman Empire escaping persecution in their own lands. The hideous political instrument we now know as 'ethnic cleansing' was formulated and formalised by the allies and the League of Nations after World War I at the Treaty of Lausanne, which ended Greece's disastrous attempt to invade modern day Turkey. At least 1.3 million Greeks were thrown out of Asia Minor. Half a million Turks or other Muslims were booted out of Greece. Communities which had lived in peace for millennia were torn apart and whole worlds destroyed. Both before and after Lausanne, Skopje was experiencing this phenomenon as Turks, Greeks, Bulgars and others left or were forcibly removed to 'their' lands.

In a precursor to the Great War, Greece, Bulgaria and Serbia joined forces to kick the Ottoman Turks out of Europe in a brutal conflict – then fell out with each other over the spoils, the geographical territory of Macedonia. In the end, the Bulgarians were defeated by a Serbian-Greek-Romanian-Montenegrin alliance and were left with only crumbs of the territory they coveted. Greece and Serbia divided up the rest between them, Greece taking the multicultural port of Salonika, Serbia grabbing a square chunk corresponding, more or less, to the current borders of Macedonia. These were victors' borders with short shrift given to the feelings of people stuck outside their homeland.

Huge population movements took place across the region during these times, and there were anomalies, such as why one third of the Albanian population was left outside the borders of the new Albanian state, in Kosovo, northern Greece and here in Macedonia.

Nobody was quite sure who those strange Slav people who predominated in Skopje were, though. They're *us*, said the Serbs, they just haven't realised it yet. No they're not, retorted the Bulgarians, they're *us*, they just need to be educated of that fact.

And some of these odd misfits had started speaking up, in what must have been one of the most mild-mannered national awakenings of all time. 'No, we're not you, or you,' they said. 'We're *us*.'

'And who exactly is that?' demanded their neighbours.

'Well we're us, and we live in Macedonia. So I guess that makes us Macedonians,' they reasoned, not unreasonably.

'Not on your bloody nelly!' cried the Greeks. 'We are the true Macedonians. You absolutely can't be.'

And this, tediously and dangerously, one hundred years on, is the problem which the Macedonian Macedonians have been facing pretty much ever since then. Ouch... my head hurts. Let's come back to this later.

The bazaar, which unexpectedly houses the city's two gay bars (that's a lot for this part of the world), is a fine and safe place to wander around day or night. That's not to say it's sterile. I definitely feel an edge when I'm wandering around. And the call to prayer does somewhat jar with the bars full of drunk revellers which sit side-by-side with hookah bars selling only soft drinks. Everybody seems to be rubbing along reasonably enough in their Balkan way. It just feels a little strange. And there are lots and lots of young men sitting around looking vaguely sullen with not very much to do.

I pop into a bar for a coffee but it's a bit more down at heel than it looked from the outside. As I'm talking to the café owner, the penny drops – the bit that nobody actually really says out loud and none of the guidebooks really address. This is the Muslim side of the river, largely Albanian with a smattering of leftover Turks, and the other side, with the statues and the statuesque blondes is the Christian part of town. It's rare to see two populations so utterly physically divided, reminiscent of Belfast maybe. Even in Riga and Tallinn, Latvians and Estonians live cheek by jowl with Russians, albeit they don't exactly get along that fantastically. Suspicion has remained between the two communities since Macedonia peacefully left Yugoslavia in 1991 (the only part to achieve this feat). Ten years later, fighting broke out with Albanians who did not want to be part of the new state and who had often been treated harshly under the old regime. Civil war threatened but a peace accord saw the Albanians guaranteed a place in any governing coalition and a proportion of jobs within the civil service. The redevelopment of Skopje has also opened old wounds, but the Macedonian government has (some say) belatedly ensured that there are Albanian national heroes among the gazillions of statues. You hope that maybe wealth could heal the wounds between these two communities, but the creation of an independent Kosovo, plus the Russian annexation of Crimea, means European borders, sacrosanct for decades since World War II, are once again being redrawn. The Albanians here know this and it's a disincentive to build a life within the Macedonian state. Many of the local Slavs believe they want the dismemberment of this Balkan chunk.

'We are Albanian,' Ali the barman tells me. 'Everybody here is Albanian. We live here and they live there.'

'They?'

'The Macedonians. They are wicked people.'

'But I have seen plenty walking about on this side...'

'They are welcomed here but we are not welcomed on their side,' he says.

I have no way of knowing if this is true. I suspect, like most dangerous exaggerations, it contains more than a grain of truth but falls far short of the actual reality.

'There will be trouble soon unless things change,' he tells me. I tell him I hope not, because I like Skopje very much and all of its people.

He softens a little, looking slightly embarrassed for his earlier comments.

'There are bad people on both sides. People who will make trouble...'

I don't doubt it, I tell him.

'But there are bad people everywhere. British troublemakers, Australian ones,' he goes on.

'Exactly,' I say. 'And so we need to make sure us nice people stick together, right?' He nods and smiles and waves me on.

It seems to me that lads like Ali are not the problem. But there are many here on all sides who could become that problem, if those old-fashioned Balkan troublemakers grab the main stage. And there are plenty living not too many miles away who wouldn't mind seeing a bit of strife in Skopje.

I head back across the river to a bar themed on London, feeling slightly dizzy and disoriented by all this experiencing. I walk through a giant red British telephone box into a bar decked out with giant Union Jacks and pictures of Amy, Jagger and the Queen. I start to fill up. Are they tears of pride? Am I missing home already? I'm ridiculous! I'm delirious. I've only been away two and a half days. But maybe it's a response to what I've just seen. You see, I live in the best place in the world. It's called Leytonstone. It doesn't know it, but really it's the heir to all those once-incredible, beautiful Balkan cities which have been 'ethnically cleansed' in the last century or so. No one group predominates in Leytonstone: British, Indians, Pakistanis, Jamaicans, Poles, Lithuanians, Algerians and South Africans – even the odd Geordie – everybody gets along. There is a respect for otherness which I never felt growing up in the North East. Wherever we have come from in the world, in Leytonstone we all, after a few months, identify as Londoners and more particularly Leytonstonians.

Next night I head to Forza Café and Bar, reputedly Skopje's finest eatery in the unlikely surroundings of a sports centre on the outskirts of town. Macedonian food is delicious, though I've already been warned by Macedonia's Ambassador to London that there really is no such thing as Macedonian cuisine.

'If you go into a café in Skopje they will serve you a Macedonian coffee. It's exactly the same as a Turkish coffee,' he smiles wryly.

'Macedonia, Serbia, Greece, Bulgaria, Turkey, Albania – they will all tell you about their national cuisines, but really it's the food of the Ottoman Empire.' From the gates of Budapest to the Red Sea, the Caucasus and the Persian Gulf, foods were swapped between massively diverse cultures to create a broadly similar cuisine which is invariably exquisite, and Macedonia is no exception. The *burek*, a sweaty heap of melting filo pastry filled with salty cheese or ground lamb and onions, may well be their national dish – though the Turks claim it as their own. The national condiment, *ajvar*, is absolutely Macedonian in origin, though you will find it everywhere throughout the Balkans. Traditionally made at home in the kitchen from pounds and pounds of huge, juicy, local red peppers stewed down to a paste and mixed with aubergine, garlic and chilli, if you can get it fresh, served with the barbecued meats they do so well here in Macedonia, you will be in heaven.

At Forza, I meet chef Vlatko Ognenovski, the country's most celebrated culinary wunderkind, larger than life and made-for-television. As well as a dinner of chicken with local ceps, ginger, tomatoes and white wine, he proffers cheeses and wines which could hold their own among the finest in the world. Who knew? I try a cheese which would make a fine pecorino taste like Mini Babybel. The local wines, grown under constant summer sunshine from the unique Stanuchina grape and weighing in at a hefty 14.5 per cent alcohol, have a smoky, mellow gravitas that would make you place them around Puglia, not the heart of the Balkans.

Ognenovski, once a personal chef to the very rich and famous, has been hired by the government to front a new Jamie Oliver-style show on local television, where he zips around the glorious Macedonian countryside with a load of plebeian city dwellers, teaching them about their country's food heritage, its abundance of tomatoes, apples, wild herbs, berries, cheeses, wines and free-range meats that really do make the country a food-lover's paradise. Like the tsunami of new-old buildings, it's a project designed to instil pride and identity in a new nation which is still finding its feet.

Later, I wander around town and end up in a Russian-managed bar, done up to look like the Sistine Chapel. They're fond of a theme in Skopje and they aren't afraid of overstatement.

Now there's dour and there's dour. And there's Russian. Russians don't particularly care if you love them or not and because of a history of fear and pain and intense suffering, do not like to show their emotions in public. That would betray weakness. Behind closed doors these people will laugh and smile and treat you like family. Their look is designed to be what it is: a facial demeanour which neither gives nor desires affirmation. It's quite extraordinary to me, an actual Geordie. In this strange, plastic Italianate bar populated by stereotypical Slavs, you do wonder if you are in the company of sociopaths. The men in this bar are wrestler-esque in their demeanour. The women exhibit a cold-eyed brassiness which would make Madonna look like, well, the other madonna. I encountered a similar thing once in Croatia, where despite the physical beauty, I felt as if I were heading for a breakdown from not hearing people laugh, from smiling at people who don't smile back. They're lovely, kind people but they have perfected the art of the resting bitch face. They must think the British and Americans are absolute grinning weirdos.

The next day I'm in a strange café, down by the river doing a bit of writing and listening to Macedonian lounge cover versions – not by choice, I hasten to add. You'll hear a lot of lounge cover versions in Skopje. You could say they have gone lounge cover version crazy. The singers deliver minimal emotion, sounding like they are morphined up to the eyeballs. I think that's how Macedonia likes its chanteuses. I've just heard a lounge cover version of New Order's *Bizarre Love Triangle*. Before that was Beyonce's *Crazy in Love*. And now it's Bon Jovi's *Living on a Prayer*. They've even done a version of Prodigy's *Firestarter*. OK, that last one was a lie. As far as I'm aware. They all sound exactly like the last. Like the singer lost the will to live several years ago and is just medicating herself through to the end of her days, twisting her hair desperately around her finger as she vaguely bothers to sing. They even do lounge cover versions of songs which were already lounge, like *The Girl from Ipanema* or *Do You Know the Way to San Jose*, only drained of any original joy. Skopje makes me smile because and not in spite of this. It's such an otherworldly place.

Back at the hotel, they've arranged for me to have an hour with Natasha, their on-call masseuse. I've been feeling under the weather for a couple of days, not at my best. My joints are aching, my sciatica has suddenly kicked in and I'm feeling sleepy every couple of hours. I'm panicking that I'm about to get ill just as I'm on my first leg of my odyssey. That would be a nightmare and I'm mainlining Berocca and Boots' Cold and Flu Defence.

Natasha is everything I want her to be. She's five-foot-nowt with a jet black bob, bright red lippie, shoulders like Christmas turkeys and hands like hams. She climbs on top of me and pummels me ferociously for an hour of pure bliss and pain. Every time an ache shifts from one part of my body to another, she instinctively finds it and beats it out of me. '*Dobra*?' ('Yes?') she asks me whenever she finds a new pressure point. '*Dobra*! *Dobra*!' I pant and beg. 'Oh bloody hell yes *dobra*!' By the end of my hour, my back has gone from the consistency of old overcooked mutton to pizza dough. The fee is 15 euros, which is frankly ridiculous, so I pay her 25 and still feel bad for exploiting her. She shrieks with joy and instinctively cuddles me. I hold on for a second or two too long, and feel a tear drop down my cheek onto her red silk blouse. Oh dear, I'm three days in and I'm having a breakdown already, I think. Still, it feels good to be held.

On a sunny final morning in Skopje, I go for one final wander around its extraordinary new centre. I check out the new National Theatre, on the spot where the old one disappeared in the earthquake, and it's genuinely a lovely and romantic spot, as evinced by a local couple who are having their wedding pictures taken outside. And you know what I reckon? All beautiful old cities were new once. Who knows, maybe when the Bohemians built Prague, the Moravians and the Cracovians and the Transylvanians were all sniggering behind their hands going, 'Ooh, have you seen the state of Prague? I mean it's just SO ostentatious. How nouveau riche can you get?' When Macedonia left Yugoslavia it was a country desperately searching for an identity. It is a nation that needs that reassurance, surrounded by countries which are at best unhelpful, at worst downright hostile. The citizens of two of its neighbours (at least), Albania and Kosovo, would happily see it dismembered. Serbians have still not forgiven it for quitting Yugoslavia and in many cases doubt its actual existence as a nation; Bulgarians just think Macedonians are deluded Bulgarians waiting to come home. And the Greeks? Well the Greeks just fume and pretend to the world (and themselves) that this tiny chunk of the Balkans is a threat to its territorial integrity. The upshot is that the Macedonian desire to be welcomed into NATO or the EU is further away than ever from being fulfilled. There is a dangerous vacuum at the heart of the Balkans ready to be exploited by Islamists, nationalists or neighbours with malign intentions. It was a miracle that Macedonia escaped most of the bloodletting that came with the demise of Yugoslavia, a bloody miracle given its geography. It needs more support if this fine city of Skopje is not to one day go the way of some of its neighbours. Russia is busy creating merry hell on NATO's borders and after Crimea, Macedonia could be a tempting prospect for Putin.

I head back to my hotel patio and ask the waiter if I can please have a table, as I intend to munch on pizza slathered with *ajvar* and local cheese and meats while I wait for my taxi to take me to Skopje airport.

He looks panicked. 'You want table tennis?'

I crack up laughing. 'No of course I don't want table tennis,' I tell him. 'Why on earth would I be asking you for that?'

He collapses in giggles and every time he comes past my table he mimes a nifty ping-pong move at me. I like the people of this city; they're as eccentric as its architecture.

As I walk to my cab the driver waits by the river gazing at my favourite statue. It's yet another warrior on a horse (there's a lot of them about). From the opposite side of the river, he does indeed look valiant, like he's riding to the rescue. From the hotel, however, all you can see is a giant (male) horse's arse. Without being too graphic,

I will point out that said horse is anatomically accurate. I point it out to the driver and we both start laughing hysterically.

'They might have built him with his tail down,' says the driver, knowingly. Good point, well made.

Rome may have not been built in a day, but it's an extraordinary tribute to the artisans, sculptors, bridge builders and architects of Skopje that they managed to build this Balkan beauty in five years. Well, at least I think it's beautiful. And that is in the eye of the beholder, right? Like Bosnia before it, Macedonia lacks a strong sense of national identity, and that's what all these palaces, turrets, bridges and statues are about. Bosnia didn't know what it was, and so that odd little ethnic giraffe of a country was torn limb-from-limb by the jackals of competing nationalisms. Skopje could so easily have become Sarajevo. Facing more enemies than even Bosnia did, it still could be. Yes, the critics of Skopje are correct, there is bombast in this city's new architecture, but it's a bombast borne of fear and fragility and I do find that beautiful. This is a city and a country being built to last. For its sake, and for the sake of its Balkan neighbours, and all of Europe, I truly hope that it does.

BEING BEYONCE

Shakira's got it. Beyoncé has it. Biggins hasn't. But have you? To put it simply, the more flexible you can be, the cheaper your flights, and potentially the more unique and interesting your adventure is going to be.

So, let's crunch some numbers. Let's say I want to fly from London to New York on 18th January for one week. After that, on the 25th I want to fly to Los Angeles for another week. And then home. And all flights must be direct. And I don't want any flights leaving before 9a.m.or arriving after 7p.m.

Skyscanner is usually the best website if you are looking for the cheapest deals out there. So let's start our search there. I immediately find a great deal direct with Norwegian from Gatwick leaving at 5.10 p.m. and landing at JFK just after 8 p.m. for £269. That's a good price considering we had so little flexibility. A week later there's a flight from the Big Apple to LAX for just £83 – but that involves a stop at Minneapolis for an hour and a half. We're too inflexible for that, so that's out. That means the next best flight is with Delta, leaving at 11.05 a.m., for a very reasonable £105. So far, pretty darn cheap. Lastly a week later we want a direct flight back to London on Monday 1st February. We have an amazing deal with Air New Zealand, who I love, for £252; which brings us a grand total of £626 flying coast to coast for two weeks. That's a bloody good deal for an inflexible flier, but I'm booking around the right time before flying, so we're getting some of the best deals out there (check out the chapter on timing: using my 18-day rule, the flight to New York would be £30 cheaper at £239).

However, trying the same thing with flexibility, what can we come up with?

Kiwi.com currently allows for the most flexible search – so you can look to fly to a whole country, rather than back and forth searching individual cities. It would get even more gold stars from me if it allowed us to search an entire continent, but they will get there. Likewise, Kiwi.com allows you to look for the cheapest flight over an entire month or longer. This is where the real bargains begin to unfurl themselves. So let's try a search for the whole month of January, from London to anywhere in the USA, with no limit on changes. Now we find a route to New York via Copenhagen for £128, with a four hour wait in Copenhagen, on 28th January. Not too shabby. But looking further down the list, there is a 36-hour trip to NYC two days earlier for the same price. Why would you do that? Because you get a full 24 hours or 48 hours in the glorious Danish capital. So fly out across the Atlantic for half the price and treat yourself to a European mini-break into the bargain.

Now we need to look for flights to the West Coast that leave us with a decent amount of time in New York. But before we do that, let's see where the cheapest flights back to London are from, around 9–15 days after we set off. That way, we can tailor our internal flights to the best value return trip, keeping costs as low as possible. So I'm searching for anywhere in the USA to London from 11th–15th February. And here we have a real deal, Fort Lauderdale in sunny Florida for just £110. Wow. On Friday 12th February. And that's a direct, 8-hour flight.

If we ditch the Los Angeles leg, and just make it a Copenhagen–NYC–Fort Lauderdale three-centre holiday, that leaves us with just a flight from NYC to FL to find. So let's search from the 2nd–6th February. There are a whole bunch of flights with Spirit Airlines for £32. So assuming we leave New York for Florida on 6th February, here's our very appealing itinerary:

26th January	London–Copenhagen
28th January	Copenhagen–NYC
6th February	NYC–Fort Lauderdale
12th February	Fort Lauderdale–London

Total cost: £270 for return transatlantic flights and a three-centre holiday, with a bit of sunshine thrown in. That's as opposed to £626 for our non-flexible, two-centre transatlantic trip, which was in itself pretty cheap. That's a 57 per cent saving. In fact, the whole trip is only £1 more expensive than the outbound flight on our first route.

This was a cursory search using arbitrary dates. I have absolutely no doubt that with more research there are better deals than that. And if you fancy spending your savings on a few more stops across the USA, Mexico, Canada or beyond there are myriad other options. We will get you your own North America, multi-centre jaunt later in the book. But for now, remember, flexibility is your friend.

And a flexible mind will reap you the greatest travel treats of all. As I discovered...

CHAPTER 3

OFF MY TITS ON TRAMADOL IN GIRONA

Diesel and paprika. I love the smell of big Spanish cities.

After the constant exoticism of Skopje, there is something reassuring about arriving in Spain and it's strange but I feel like I've come home. I've spent more time in Spain than any other foreign state; I've had some of the happiest and saddest days of my life here. I've been in love, out of love, found out my dad was dead after a night on the tiles in Madrid – still probably my favourite city in the world outside of my home town. But now, I'm arriving in Barcelona, so I'm not just in Spain: I'm in Catalonia.

It's also reassuring to be back in a big metropolis. An adopted Londoner, I spent three years scratching my head and struggling to survive or stay sane in The Smoke before falling in love with it. I think loving London is a bit like Stockholm Syndrome, where you fall in love with your captor, and I totally understand why Londonophobes and London-sceptics are baffled by it. But it is the sense of endless possibility, the sense that anything could happen at any time, the sense that in London the only thing which limits you is your imagination, which is so addictive. Barcelona has that similar feel and I trot out of my very reasonably priced boutique hotel, the NH Eixample, excited by what the next twenty-four hours will bring. The hotel is part of a chain, NH Hotels, which is a bit like a group of Spanish Travelodges. Being Spanish, this naturally makes them a lot lovelier and more stylish than a Travelodge and means they are built in places you might actually want to wake up in.

I'm actually a bit overexcited, and plonk myself down in a Galician tapas bar just around the corner where Spanish people make that loud, lovely, clacking Spanish talking sound that they make. This gets me even more excited. Come to think of it though, am I allowed to call these people Spanish? Is this Spain? Was it ever? They're Catalan now, right? And they might be completely independent by the next time I visit. Still, forgive me Catalonian people, but you do make a loud clacking sound which is remarkably similar to the one that Spanish people make. And your cities smell of paprika and diesel, just like theirs do.

I've always wanted to try Galician food – but mine host regards me with a weary half-smile. He's probably just ready to put his feet up, but in my infinite wisdom I decide he's thinking, 'Oh, another idiot Brit, here for his fix of chicken and chips.' I'll show him. The menu is, of course, entirely in Catalan but I resolve to order from the Galician specialties. I manage to decipher the word octopus and recall the delectable baby octopus salad I had a few years back in Portugal.

'I'll have that,' I tell him. He appears to raise an eyebrow, presumably in recognition of my non-plebbishness and scuttles back to the kitchen.

A worryingly few minutes later he emerges and proudly plonks down what looks like a huge heaped plate of white blancmange, covered with something grey, leathery and smothered in suckers. It's missing the solo blinking eye, but apart from that, it seems basically to be an octopus autopsy, an octopsy. Bleughh. I feel a small amount of sick come up through my gullet and into my throat. 'Oh wow!' I say, like you do when someone reads you their own bad poetry unexpectedly and then searches your face to see if you really liked it. And you didn't. Mine host looks fondly at the octopsy as one might contemplate a favourite granddaughter or prize whippet. He mumbles something which I translate as meaning 'This is a delicious specialty, I hope you enjoy!' And then he stays there. He stays there, stood standing, awaiting my first mouthful of this quivering, smelly pile of dismembered octopus. Something resembling pus dribbles out of one of its suckers and down its flabby, fatty underskirt. It's fair to say, this is nothing like my delicious Portuguese baby octopus salad in vinaigrette.

'Oh Christ,' I say, rictus grin still etched across my face. 'Yum!' I carve a slice, well I say carve, it's more like fashioning lard, around the size of four postage stamps, from the dead cephalopod. And then I cut that in two. And I place it in my mouth. I lean over my plate to disguise a gag. It tastes… It tastes actually just of paprika and salt and sea. But the texture – the texture is the stuff of nightmares, wet and chewy and oozing and slimy and unctuous. I surprise myself by swallowing it down without barfing over the entire restaurant.

'Oh wow! Wow! Wow!' I say, which is not fundamentally insincere. Please don't stay to watch me take another bite, I silently pray. He totters back to the kitchen, I think not entirely convinced.

I manage to pile a good two thirds in a toiletries bag I picked up at Luton Airport. Outside the restaurant I dump the still-wobbling bag of congealed octopus in a bin and head off into the Barcelona night, unfed but no longer hungry.

The next day, I'm trundling through the backstreets of Barcelona to Sants Station. I've allowed myself four days in Catalonia but opted to devote just the one night to the Catalan capital. The weather is grey and the road to the station is, well, frankly ugly. Barcelona, in case you didn't know, was the birthplace of the modern PR industry; proof that with the right publicity you really can polish a turd. OK, so it's not that bad, but I think since it snagged the Olympics back in 1992, it has enjoyed a reputation way in excess of its charms. I reckon it's Europe's most overrated capital city, a few flashes of brilliance never coming close to compensating for the miles of bleakness. It's more than a bit full of itself and has none of the joie de vivre of its hated rival Madrid. It's a tribute to that incredible PR trick that millions of Brits every year bypass cities like the Spanish capital, Malaga, Valencia, Seville – I could list another 15 or 20 – in favour of Iberia's answer to Dundee. I know, I know... I'm exaggerating... But I hope you take my point. My £15 flight from the Balkans was well worth it, though, because there is far more to Catalonia than ropey Barça, and I'm off to spend my next night in one of the Mediterranean's most joyful, elegant and effortlessly chic cities, less than half an hour away.

Almost the minute my train pulls out, the clouds disperse and I'm treated to a glorious tour of the sparkling Catalan coast south of Barcelona; the mid-afternoon September sunshine turns the Mediterranean into a deep golden pond as our train rattles at breakneck speed along lethal cliff edges and over deserted sandy bays. It's such a lovely journey I almost wish the train would slow down, but I'm looking forward to getting to Sitges, which could possibly be my favourite place in the world outside Leytonstone.

Sitges is classified as a gay resort, but it's so much more than that; infinitely classier than the heaving, druggy fleshpots of Gran Canaria or Torremolinos, so much more fun than snooty, dead-behind-the-eyes Mykonos. It's full of Catalan families playing on the golden sands with their buckets and spades, European foodies entranced by one of the Med's most enchanting dining destinations, fans of art and architecture. And people who just want to chill. That's the first thing you notice about Sitges: it's just really chilled. The air is clean, the seafood is unsurpassable, the drinks are cheap and everyone seems, well, happy. Thoughts of a Spanish recession which have left horrific levels of unemployment seem a million miles away from this spangly fishing port. I sit outside Parrots Pub and Terrace for a good hour, watching the world go by and booking flights for later in my trip. Everyone in Sitges ends up sitting outside Parrots at some point; it's extremely straight-friendly, unless of course you don't like same-sex affection, in which case... don't go to Sitges. I find a pintxo bar up the hill near my lovely, boutiquey, super-cheap Hotel Galeon, and gorge on bite-sized slices of crusty bread topped with Serrano ham, manchego and *piquillo* peppers, or juicy, fat prawns on a bed of melting, creamy Cabrales blue cheese from Asturias. This almost makes up for the octopus. I go to bed a happy man. I wake up in abject agony.

The tiredness and strange achiness which I had been feeling has turned into glandular swelling. Meanwhile, my sore gums, which I have been treating with Bonjela, have swollen up massively at one side of my mouth. I know what it is. I have an infected wisdom tooth, the same tooth that nearly wrecked my visit to Bratislava in 1991. Except then it was two infected wisdom teeth. It happens sometimes when I fly. Don't ask me why. This was my biggest fear, before I set off, that this rogue tooth would wreck my plan to fly to ten cities. Why haven't I had it removed, I hear you ask? Well, it only flares up once in a blue moon and it's been fairly well behaved of late. I had the other one done, not long after returning from Bratislava. I was skint, so I went to the dental hospital. I had a student drilling into my face for an hour while I was fully conscious and the painkillers really weren't having the desired effect. When he had finished he turned to my right side and prepared to launch himself at my other rogue molar.

'Glagh aagh aagh aagh agh!' I told him, waving my arms vociferously, which translated as 'Don't you fucking dare, mate!' I could barely eat or speak and bled orally for two weeks solid. I have suffered bereavements which have caused me less distress. So that's why I never got it sorted. I have heard tell that things have moved on somewhat since I was half murdered by the Sweeney Todd of dentistry. But this terrible ache makes me rethink my decision. I am loaded on paracetamol, codeine, ibuprofen, aspirin, something I've been given for my back, Bonjela... but I am still in agony. It has to be stopped. Inside my mouth there is a huge swelling, a pillow of bloated gum not dissimilar to the octopus of Barcelona. The internet tells me this is an abscess. Full of infection. What do we do with abscesses? We wait for them to burst, it tells me. Not on your nelly. One American website has the answer. Skip some pages now if you're squeamish. It reads, 'Lancing your own abscess'.' There's no stopping me. I am a man possessed. By pain. I march down to reception and demand a sewing kit, then 200 yards to the chemist where I buy various bottles of antiseptic for sterilising equipment. And then I perform minor dental surgery upon myself.

Readers, I am not recommending you try this at home. What I did was probably highly dangerous and irresponsible, not least if my hand had slipped and I had swallowed the needle.

In the end, I have the needle so deeply embedded in my gum abscess, I have to yank it out of my face. There are actually several of these putrid boils, and by the time I have finished, I have made around six punctures in this alien mouth invader. Having finished stabbing at it, I then have to squeeze hard and let the foul tasting liquid within ooze out. My hotel bathroom looks like someone has performed an 'octopsy' in it. I wet wipe, empty an entire tube of Bonjela over my deflated abscess, take another six painkillers, pack quickly, and leg it down to breakfast. I have ten minutes before they finish serving and am experiencing that strange sense of euphoria you feel in the aftermath of intense pain. I am unstoppable. I'm glad I make it. My stay at the Galeon has cost £40 for a beautiful room and a breakfast which is really brunch. As well as amazing yoghurts filled with fresh fruits and granola, there are all the British breakfast classics cooked well, several types of egg, salads with hams, king prawns and smoked salmon, about five stews, roast chicken, spare ribs… basically anything you could possibly want, plus freshly squeezed juices, every kind of coffee and unlimited cava for those not afraid to drink before noon on their holidays. The hotel is smack bang in the centre of old Sitges, it's peaceful and there's a lovely pool and jacuzzi area. After a breakfast like that you don't need to eat again until dinner. If you're going to Sitges, and you really should if you're in this neck of the woods, I could not endorse anywhere more highly. This is a good, honest hotel in a good, honest town. Even with a giant abscess, it's a pleasure.

Juggling 11 flights in 30 days, there are always going to be cock-ups but my first major booking mistake turned into a happy accident.

If you are booking a budget trip around the world, it is worth noting that some airports are nowhere near where the airlines say they are (*see* page 117). Ryanair have particular form for this, and it can make a budget trip turn out to be not as budget as you first hoped. Paris Vatry Airport for instance is a whopping 162 kilometers – over 100 miles – from the centre of the French capital. It is, however, bang in the middle of the champagne region. Surely if they were to rename it Champagne Airport it would not only be more honest but also the most alluring airport in the world? I think we can forgive London Stansted because of its excellent and reasonably priced links to the English capital, but London Oxford Airport is, frankly, taking the piss. So booking my flight out of Barcelona, I leapt at a bargain journey to another exotic hotspot, without noticing that it was taking off from 'Barcelona Girona' Airport, which is, in truth, Girona Airport. It's understandable why they would want to cash in on the hype surrounding Barcelona, but what a slap in the face for Girona, one of Europe's most ancient and beautiful cities. Millions of tourists rush on to the fast train south to Barça and bypass Catalonia's loveliest and most Catalan city. The locals must be so offended; or perhaps they are happy to keep this iridescent jewel of a town all to themselves. Frankly, it's like climbing over Princess Diana to get to Camilla Parker Bowles.

I missed my train trying to use the nonsensical ticket machines at Barcelona Sants (Clue: nobody else was using them. Tip: Go straight to the booking desk or buy online) but actually the station was a far from unpleasant place to hang out in for an hour while I waited to catch the fast train to Paris, which hits Girona after a mere 35 minutes. I drank silky macchiato, and ate a gourmet *bocadillo* on leather banquettes before jumping into a soft, air-conditioned seat on a two-storey train. I love travelling on Spanish trains, though they make me shiver with embarrassment at the state of British railways. God knows how they paid for it. Presumably instead of spending their time in the EU nitpicking and carping from the sidelines, like Britain does, they got stuck in and worked it for every penny they could get. And if they did, good for them. Or maybe that's why they nearly went bankrupt. Who knows, but when the Spanish economy inevitably recovers, they will have a reasonably priced, modern, comfortable and efficient transport infrastructure equipped for the 21st century. I love my country but its inability to provide basic services at a fair price to its hard-working people is a national shame. We invented the railways, for goodness' sake.

Soon I was gliding regally out of Barcelona once more and into the verdant, sun-drenched Catalan countryside. What you see before you is a bona fide land of plenty – rolling hills, castles, mountains, lakes, still unspoiled. One of the many vows I made on this trip was to find time to come back and explore Catalonia's abundant green valleys and vineyards. This is a land apart from Spain's deep, dusty and dusky south.

I'm staying at the hyper-stylish Gran Ultonia, just outside the Old Town. I'm fighting grumpiness because of my enduring mouth pain, but my junior suite is pure, modern, Catalan cool, bright and white with a bed bigger than my London flat, chaise longue, dreamy mood lighting, massive bathroom and changing area with walk-in shower. The atmosphere is understated urban glamour – basically the opposite of any W Hotel, if you've ever stayed in one. I dose myself up on more painkillers and Bonjela and head to Plaça de la Independència, where I manage to eat a sublime steak with blue cheese of such tenderness that even my poorly mouth can cope. It's not by accident that Girona is home to the world's most famous and arguably best restaurant, El Bulli, and this bewitching little city can fairly lay claim to being the gastronomic capital of Catalonia.

A walk around the blissfully quiet streets of the Old Town eases my pain. At times you feel like you have this city to yourself as you clip-clop through hushed, ancient, cobbled streets, then you sporadically come upon a bar or restaurant that is packed and bustling. I debate the independence issue with a few locals in a bar, who are fascinated to know about the Scottish referendum. Unlike Scotland, Catalonia is not constitutionally allowed a referendum on independence from Spain. The state insists that the nation is indivisible, and so the nationalist parties declared regional elections a de facto referendum on independence. The result was a disaster for everyone, with the nationalists winning a majority of seats, but less than half of the vote. The Catalan governing coalition has declared itself free of the Spanish constitutional court and is taking steps to create separate public bodies from Spain. The national government is saying, 'No way, José!' There's a dangerous stand-off. Madrid fears, realistically, that if it allows Catalonia a true referendum on independence, then the Basques, the Galicians, the Andalusians and others will want the same rights. If Catalonia leaves, then the Balkanisation of Iberia will begin. Strewth. This is a complicated continent. Around Girona there are little emblems everywhere proclaiming that Catalonia is not Spain. The people I speak to seem angry that they have not got the same rights as Scots, but the Scottish referendum hardly ended the rancour between nationalists and unionists. You suspect that the anti-independence Catalans, as in Scotland, find it harder to speak out – but the fact is, the independence parties got less than half of the vote. Even if they had a referendum, even if the separatists got 51 per cent of the vote, would that really confer legitimacy on the dissolution of an arrangement which has lasted for hundreds of years, ruled the world, and made itself one of the world's predominant cultures, far ahead of bigger, stronger, France, Germany or Russia for instance? As with Scotland and the UK, Spain and Catalonia are like a mildly disgruntled couple wanting a bit more from their lives and blaming their spouse for holding them back. Every other Wednesday they meet to decide on divorce. Usually they say no. Then one month, inevitably, by 51 to 49 per cent, they say yes and it's over. There is no way back. No second thoughts.

Scottish and Catalan nationalists are the cool kids, not like their old fogey rivals preserving the status quo. But there was nothing cool about the nationalists of the Balkans 100 years ago. Yugoslavia was a dead rubber, unloved and unwanted by anyone, but it mostly prevented the bloodletting that ensued after its break up. The Union of Soviet Socialist Republics was not socialist and never a union. But Spain and Great Britain have endured through thick and thin, and 51 per cent does not strike me as the resounding 'yes' to independence from a people who have been subjugated and repressed such as the Estonians or the Kosovans. It sounds like a people mildly bored by the current set-up. The Spanish government's stubborn inability to allow the Catalans a true referendum increases nationalist support day by day. And yes, inevitably, Catalonia will one day leave Spain and Scotland will leave Britain. When I discuss this with my Catalan friends, the best and most persistent argument they can come up with is that independence was 'a matter of national pride'. Well of course it flipping is, because it makes no sense in any other than an emotional way. The Estonians didn't escape the Soviet Union because of national pride; they did it because their culture and nationality was being slowly and deliberately annihilated; Kosovo escaped Serbia because the population were victims of actual genocide. Let's put Catalonia's 'pride' issues into context.

I climb into bed as the mouth pain also climbs. I neck a few more painkillers, lost count now, but nothing seems to touch it. At half past midnight I wake up and it's unbearable so I reach for my nuclear option. A Tramadol. An opiate. Which basically means it's laboratory-created heroin. Don't ask me how I got my hands on it. OK, do. I found a silver pack of four outside a newsagent in Leytonstone. Someone had dropped them. I thought: 'Wooh, Tramadol, I've heard of that and I seem to remember it's something quite good.' Weeks later I put my back out (I know, I'm a wreck) and my friend gave me one of her Tramadol while we were out and about and I went from looking like Edvard Munch's *The Scream* to Garfield. Totally blissed out. I am in no way endorsing the use of unprescribed drugs but my God, I needed it. Not even stopping to think about any repercussions, I guzzle the Tramadol, and within a few minutes I have sunk into a womb-like state of sleep.

A few hours later I wake up in a room with the lights blazing. For a few moments I can't remember who I am, then when I do, all I can think is where the fuck am I? This is only my fourth city but I am utterly confused. I walk around my bright white suite with literally no idea where I am or what I am doing there. I'm starting to panic and the more I try to concentrate to work out where I am, the more the answer eludes me. I WhatsApp my friend in America and ask him where I am. Weirdly, even though my brain doesn't know where it is, it knows what WhatsApp is and that my friend will still be up because it's early evening where he is. He tells me I'm in Girona, and I throw myself back on the bed in relief. The pain is back in full force. I neck another Tramadol and pass out once more.

My hotel phone wakes me up at 9.30 a.m. 'Your tour guide has been waiting downstairs for an hour, Mr Fraser.' Oh bollocks. I run downstairs and meet her.

'Oh my goodness – your face,' she says, wincing.

The right hand side is about 30 per cent bigger than the left hand side. I look like the elephant man. She whisks me to a dentist who X-rays me, identifies a massive sac of infection behind my wisdom tooth, and loads me up with more sensible painkillers and antibiotics, plus the promise that the pain will begin to subside very soon. I'm still off my tits on Tramadol, and float through Girona's sun dappled streets and back to my hotel. After an hour on my bed, counting to one hundred over and over while praying that the pain will subside, I take a walk through Girona's Old Town, loaded with so many painkillers I rattle, and frankly as high as a kite. It's lovely. Really lovely. And I'm not just saying that *because* I was high as a kite. If you are going to have brain-meltingly bad toothache anywhere in the world, then Girona is the place to have it. The people are lovely, the dentists are first class, the tour guides are the kindest and most understanding, the city is soporific, with a gentle beauty and a calm which, with its lazy River Onyar surrounded by gorgeous multi-coloured medieval tic-tac box houses, gives it a feel of the River Arno in Florence without the hordes, and actually more beautiful. I can't wait to go back when I'm not in abject agony.

That night I dine outside, on soft food, on the steps of a church in the city's famous Le Bistro restaurant, where tables are scattered down cobbled steps. It's a place for lovers. But I am` alone with my toothache and my thoughts. It's subsided enough for me to enjoy my meal of lamb loin stuffed with manchego followed by a dreamy baked cheesecake. Weirdly, the Tramadol seems to imbue you with a sense of floaty peace, even when you feel pain. And I think – remembering my conversation about Catalan independence – how mad this continent of Europe is. How mad we all are. How much more similar we all are than we want to admit. How incredibly beautiful it is. And how the world's smallest continent, despite our awful history, is without a doubt, the most interesting, alluring, compelling, intoxicating place on earth. Like Macedonia, and probably Catalonia, Europe is sometimes too interesting for its own good. But I feel a love for it and a belonging to it that I can't feel anywhere else in the world. It's like a great big dysfunctional Catholic family: you know that what binds you to it is more than the stuff that repels you. It's a feeling I will have many times on my trip.

TODAY DONCASTER OR LATROBE, TOMORROW THE WORLD

There are many inadvertent bonuses to tripping the flight fantastic. Of course, first and foremost, you're bagging the cheapest flights. The flights are cheaper because, let's be honest, often they are to less fashionable cities, like Girona instead of Barcelona. But of course, don't let's confuse 'less fashionable' with 'more rubbish'. I picked up a flight to one of Europe's 2016 Capitals of Culture for £3.30, so don't be fooled. Just because the self-appointed style arbiters haven't found it doesn't mean it's not amazing. And how much more exciting is it to be the first to uncover a hidden gem?

The matrix of flights across all continents is more intricate than the design of a snowflake and there are more and more cities joining the grid as old, disused airfields are rediscovered and rebranded as new hubs/destinations joining the race for tourist cash every year. Enterprising airlines and regional development agencies hook up to fly us to the back of beyond. And it works both ways. If you can find your way to some untouched crevice of Corsica, some nifty nook of Norway, then that means you can also get there from your own one-time backwater. Once upon a time, your options for international adventures were somewhat limited if you wanted to fly from your hometown airport, be it Aberdeen, Teesside, Bournemouth or Blackpool. Basically it was Benidorm or bugger all. The advent of freedom of movement in the EU jobs market hasn't just brought

Lithuanians to Leith. It also means you can travel in the opposite direction, and onwards to curiouser and curiouser climes. I like to think of *Tripping* as being like an air cruise. But unlike a cruise, you can set off from the place down the bottom of your road. And don't listen to the travel snobs who knock 'provincial' airports. Little airports are easier, cheaper, friendlier and much less hassle than their big brothers.

No longer do you have to spend a fortune getting to Gatwick or Manchester. The world's most exotic locations are a few hops away, wherever you live. Remember that game Six Degrees of Separation, where everybody in the world could be linked via Kevin Bacon? Well the same pretty much applies for budget travel. In six cheap hops you can get almost anywhere in the world from the airport at the bottom of your road. It takes a bit of research and to-ing and fro-ing until someone comes up with a search engine which will whittle down these myriad choices for you. Still, it can be worth the effort. Let's have a gander and see where we can get to from our regional hubs in the next few weeks. We'll call it Six Degrees of Doncaster Robin Hood.

Doncaster/Sheffield Robin Hood Airport has a veritable cup floweth over of sexy destinations just a quick hop and a few quid away from its base, including Gdansk, Warsaw, Wroclaw and Kosice all going for under £20. For my cheap trip around unusual climes, I'm gonna plump for the ancient Polish city of Lublin, which proffers the cheapest flight outta Donny, going for £8.88 on Tuesday 26th January. Assuming I stayed two to four nights, that would mean leaving town between 28th and 30th. Using Skyscanner's handy 'whole month' search tool, I see there's a flight to Stockholm costing £7, flying out on Saturday 30th. Can't be bad, with Stockholm also a hub city for flights all over the world – and it's a perfect 1 p.m. flight time to boot. If I hadn't plumped for the Swedish beauty, Kiwi. com tells me I could have opted for Dusseldorf, Katowice, Gdansk, Warsaw, Copenhagen or indeed Doncaster return for under £20. So that's a great short break from Doncaster for £27 return if you're not looking to meander. But so far we have spent £15 getting to Sweden via Poland. Again, assuming a two- to four-night break in Stockholm, that means flying out between 1st and 3rd February. Using Kiwi.com's excellent 'search date range' facility, I find flights to Vilnius, Warsaw, London, Wroclaw, Katowice, Brussels, Poznan and Copenhagen for under £10. For just a little more there is Budapest and Macedonia's amazing capital Skopje for under £12 and Bucharest for £15. In total Stockholm offers 52 European cities, one for every week of the year, for under £20 for those three days. See what I mean about Doncaster being the gateway to the world?

At this point, if I was carrying on with a completely budget trip, I'd grab the cheap flights from Stockholm to Skopje or Budapest, or perhaps Ancona in Italy, and head towards sunnier, more southerly climes. But Kiwi.com's excellent facility to search for an entire country makes me curious as to what's available across the pond. I type in 'United States' and up comes New York for a ridiculous £113, leaving on Monday 1st February, with Norwegian Airlines. So now I've visited three cities for £128, and I'm in New York! It's got to be three nights minimum in the Big Apple, so let's leave from 4th to 6th February. I hit the 'anywhere' button and there is Dallas, the deliciously titled Myrtle Beach, Burlington and Fort Lauderdale for under £40. Boston is a few quid more, and

I know both it and Fort Lauderdale offer cheap and convenient routes back home. Fort Lauderdale is hot and fun and a great hub for flights further on, so that's my fourth degree of separation from Doncaster, for £39 – meaning I've now spent £167 and I'm in sunny Florida, flying out on 6th February, so it's a nice long stay in New York. Staying a minimum three nights in Fort Lauderdale means I leave on 9th or 10th February, and Tuesdays and Wednesdays are great days to grab bargains. Hitting the 'anywhere' button offers me Baltimore, Tampa, Dallas and Orlando for under £30. The latter two both great hubs for flights back home. But I fancy spicing things up and £39 takes me to my fifth degree of separation from Doncaster, and let me tell you, it's a long way from Meadowhall to Mexico City. So I've spent £206 and I'm in the Mexican capital on Wednesday 10th February thanks to a four-hour flight with the local carrier Volaris. And again, these are nice afternoon flight times. Time to think about home and with a minimum stay of two nights in Mexico, I look for flights back homeward from 12th to 16th February. There are again myriad stepping stones but Kiwi.com's search, which allows travel times between cities of up to 50 hours, should enlighten me on some handy routes. London's only £218 coming back through Fort Lauderdale on 15th February, giving me plenty of time to explore Mexico City. And London can be my sixth degree of separation from Doncaster. So there you have it: £424 buys me a mind-bogglingly exotic trip around two continents, six cities and four countries. All from Doncaster Robin Hood.

Of course you may have noticed I didn't end up back in Sheffield. After a trip like that, I'm guessing most people would maybe spend a night or two in the smoke, then catch the exorbitantly-priced train back up north. If you are determined to be dropped at your doorstep, an extra £43 will give you a night in Dublin, after a night in London, arriving home in Donny at a respectable 10.25 a.m. Bobsyeruncle.

But it's not just Doncaster where you can do this from. It's the same wherever you're travelling from, and whether it's a 'provincial' airport in the UK or anywhere else. Bournemouth will take you to Barcelona and then off around the world from there. Maybe South America? Derry is a great portal to Oslo, and either off around Poland or across to North America; Aberdonian adventures will likely start in Gdansk, which is a delightful city in its own right, but also a great route to fabulous, underrated Warsaw and never boring Brussels, both great hub cities for onwards journeys around the world. Liverpool has Limoges, a brilliant gateway to France, Iberia and Italy, while Newcastle's Dublin route opens up the whole of Europe and North America as well as linking two fine Georgian cities. What self-respecting Geordie wouldn't factor in a couple of nights of good craic in the Irish capital? London and Manchester... pfft... You can stick 'em!

We can also play this game in North America: let's call it Six Degrees of Latrobe Arnold Palmer (and revert to dollars – just this once). If you are one of the dunces who, heaven forbid, hasn't heard of Latrobe, Pennsylvania, let me enlighten you. This is a city of 8,338 souls located in the bottom left corner of the Keystone State. Its mayor is a certain Ms Rosemary M Wolford, and its claim to fame is that it is the birthplace of the trumpeter Dennis Ferry (no, I'm none the wiser, either) and more promisingly the banana split which was first whipped up by one David Evans Strickler at Strickler's drug store in 1904.

Many have deigned to overlook Latrobe, Pennsylvania because it is, tragically, emasculated by its lack of a city nickname, unlike its neighbours: Punxsutawney, inexplicably garlanded as the Weather Capital of the World; Reading, the Pretzel Capital of the World; and Allentown, which greedily has declared itself to be both Peanut City and the Truck Capital of the World. Never mind, Latrobe, it could be worse: you could be Pittsburgh, who some cruel soul has damned forever as the Birmingham of America. Now that's just plain mean!

Anyway, Latrobe may well have the last laugh, after all, for it is also home to Latrobe Arnold Palmer Regional Airport. Arnold Palmer is a world-famous American golfer from the 1960s. So famous is he that he not only has an airport named after him but also a cocktail, an intriguing and ingenious blend of lemonade and iced tea, known across the globe as the Arnold Palmer. And Latrobe Arnold Palmer Regional Airport is not just a bloody mouthful but also an amazing and cheap stepping-stone to the travel hubs of Orlando and Fort Lauderdale, thanks to the wonderful Spirit Airlines.

So off we hop from Latrobe to its main hub Fort Lauderdale on Tuesday 5th April for $47 with Spirit. After four nights of Florida sun and occasional high camp, I'm guessing, $68 will take us to the Big Apple for five nights of shopping and bar-hopping on 9th April, again with Spirit.

On 14th April we hop on to a Norwegian Dreamliner, no less, as we head to serene Stockholm for $219 with Norwegian. Six nights will be spent in the Swedish capital before flying on Wednesday 20th April to Sweden's soporific southern port of Malmö with Wizz Air for $22. Don't worry if the city's not big enough to fill the days, you can always cross the Øresund Bridge into classy Copenhagen for two or three nights, before returning to Malmö to catch another Wizz Air flight to the gorgeous Transylvanian town of Cluj-Napoca, with its brooding castle and intriguing Romanian–Hungarian cultural hotchpotch, on Tuesday 26th April for $54 with Wizz Air.

A week in one of Europe's most beguiling towns will end when you fly to the breathtaking Bavarian city of Nuremberg for $28 on 3rd May. Five days later, on 8th May you leap on a Ryanair flight to must-see London for $26. Another five nights, and you're off to possibly your fourth Scandinavian bolthole, pristine Oslo, with Ryanair on 13th May, for a bargain $24.

Now it's time to head home and three nights later you're back in Fort Lauderdale, with Norwegian, for $178. Then after a one-night stand in the cheeky Florida resort, it's back to the never-ceasingly captivating Latrobe, and its trumpets and banana splits, for $47.

So to round up; that's Pennsylvania to Transylvania and beyond (Fort Lauderdale, New York, Stockholm, Malmö, Cluj-Napoca, Nuremberg, London, Oslo) and back to Latrobe for a grand price of $713, or less than most people pay for a return flight to a single European City. Eat your heart out, Punxsutawney!

Things get even better for the Latrobians; with a little flexibility you can fly from that sacred city to San Juan, Nassau, Bogota, Medellin, Mexico City and Port au Prince for less than it costs to get to nearby Allentown. Remember? The Peanut City/Truck Capital of the World. I know which I would choose.

But truth be told, it's not just Latrobe. Whether it's Detroit to Colombia, Myrtle Beach to Canada, or Denver to Mexico, in the crazy matrix of international budget flights, the world's most weird, exotic and obscure cities are but a heartbeat from the bottom of your drive.

CHAPTER 4
CATNIP TO ITALIANS

So, I'm zig-zagging back across the Mediterranean, this time the 400 miles from Girona, to pop in on Pisa. I know I'll be heading back in a few weeks to the kind of English October which saps the soul and could turn Fozzie Bear into Leonard Cohen, so I figure a few more southern hotspots won't do me any harm before I take a deep breath and give it all up for chilly northern Europe. September and October, like March and April, are good months to embark on this kind of adventure because you are spared the tourist hordes, prices are low, southern Europe is not too hot and northern Europe is not unbearably cold.

There's a lot said about low-cost airlines and particularly Ryanair, but this is a lovely flight with a surprising amount of legroom and it's half empty, so I can stretch out and snooze once we are up in the air. Both Girona and Pisa airports are small, efficient, accessible and cheap to get to from the city centre, whether you opt for taxi, bus or train. When I land, I'm struck by the similarities in landscape and architecture between these two once-powerful cities, separated by the Mediterranean and Ligurian seas.

I'm booked in the Puccini Suite at Pisa's lovely Hotel Bologna, nestling close to the bosom of this pleasantly compact and navigable Tuscan city. Decked out with antiques and wooden shutters overlooking narrow streets, there's a hush here that soothes my mind and my still-aching jaw and although I'm desperate to explore, my body is still not fighting fit. It was an early morning flight, and I've been surviving on one meal a day because of my oral problems. I take more painkillers, pray for the pain to go away and fall asleep for an hour or two on a big, soft bed.

I wake up grumpy. And become grumpier at myself for being grumpy in the middle of such an incredible experience. But if there's one thing I've learned, bullying yourself into being happy, when you're not, is not going to make things better. It's like Christmas sadness. You feel like a failure if you're miserable at Christmas or on holiday, especially on a trip like this around so many amazing places. But it wouldn't be natural to be happy for a month, unless you're mainlining ecstasy the whole time, which I really don't advise. Feel your feelings, accept them as part of human nature, even those horrible nitpicking ungrateful thoughts we all have from time to time. And then move on. Unfortunately, I'm unable to take my own advice right now, my grumpiness is turning to anger and because I am refusing to acknowledge it, it's only getting worse.

Then I pick up my phone. It's a cheap smartphone, which I get through a contract with Virgin. While I was sleeping, it downloaded a system update which basically made it forget it was a phone. I Google the problem and see that other users have had similar problems. Luckily I can still use the hotel Wi-Fi. I Google the Virgin helpdesk. There is no email address. Anywhere.

'If your phone is broken, please give us a call,' it cheerily advises. I would hopefully not need to point out the logic gap to anyone over the age of six. Aggggggghhhhhhhhhh!

If you embark on a trip like this, your phone is your lifeline, and I don't really know how you would manage these days without one: firstly for email, for flight bookings and the like; secondly for local information (you might not know exactly where you are going to visit, when you head off on your adventure); thirdly, if you're travelling alone, there is nothing better than WhatsApp-chatting with an old mate when you are feeling lost and bewildered, either by text or by their free call service. Lastly, and most importantly, satnav will save you hours wandering lost around the backstreets of Marseilles or Munich. It also saves you a fortune in taxi fares. There is nowhere you cannot access on foot in cities the size of Pisa or Girona. Satnav means you can explore as you choose, or just get deliriously lost, knowing your phone will guide you safely home. I have a phone and a tablet, but now both only work off Wi-Fi until I get my hands on Richard Branson.

I stomp into Pisa not feeling quite in the holiday mode. I go to a café and ask if I can pay on my credit card, but they don't accept them. Really? I try another one: not them neither. I need to find an ATM but I've wandered for a long while without a sniff. There is one on every corner in Girona, Skopje, London. Grrr. I scrape together enough euros for a macchiato, thinking I can connect to the café Wi-Fi and Google where to find an ATM. The café doesn't have Wi-Fi. Neither does the one next door. There is a city Wi-Fi but it never works the whole time I am here. I ask in a couple of caffs but people just shrug. I remember what I have forgotten on every visit to Italy. This country is infuriating. No ATMs, no Wi-Fi, they don't take credit cards… Oh, and half the bars don't have toilets. WTF??

After an hour of searching I find an ATM, buy more painkillers, and find a spot for lunch. I'm in one of the greatest food regions of the world, if not the greatest, Tuscany. But my tum, abused with painkillers of every flavour, antibiotics and now unused to regular food, is feeling very tender. I resolve to make myself eat, and order a bowl of Tuscan minestrone. Crushed beans and pumpkin, tomato, aubergine, carrot and spinach: a plate of simple goodness staring back at me. Although nothing tastes good when you have lost your appetite entirely, my brain and my soul appreciate that this might be the best thing I have done all day.

The restaurant proprietor, who has made me dizzy spending 15 minutes angrily telling me how all his competitors use frozen food, goes back into the restaurant as I sit by a small garden outside. Suddenly my stomach starts to lurch, and while nonchalantly pretending to inspect the leaves of a tree, I throw up violently in a bush. Oops.

I trudge back to my room where I spend half an hour fruitlessly searching for ways to speak to Virgin Media through a phone that doesn't know it's a phone. The only live link with another human being at the company is with their sign language service, where you are promised a real live moving human being when you get connected. So I feign deafness and wait for half an hour to get through. Eventually I am asked to leave a voice message and I plaintively beg for someone to get back to me on my email or WhatsApp or anywhere. They don't. I take another Tramadol and fall back to sleep.

I wake up around 8 p.m., and after showering and dressing I head out for dinner. The lovely hotel staff have given me directions to one of the best places in town but without my satnav I can't find it. I forgot to pick up a map and I can't read them anyway, so I wander fruitlessly in circles around a dark, deserted Pisan night. I go back to my hotel and they tell me the restaurant will have closed by now anyway. I'm at the end of my tether when I enter the empty restaurant around the corner from my hotel. I can feel the beginnings of something akin to hunger, but my mouth can't handle anything that needs chewing. Fortunately, I'm in the home of pasta and I order a bowl of gnocchi with wild boar ragù.

Lo and behold, the restaurant actually has Wi-Fi and a message comes through from my friend Katie. 'I bet you are having an amazing adventure,' she writes.

'No, I'm not,' I write back. 'I feel like someone has jammed a screwdriver through my ear and down into my jaw, I'm in the food capital of the world and I can't eat and that grinning idiot Richard Branson has ruined my life entirely.'

Katie knows exactly what to say. 'Well we love you and miss you and are proud of you,' she writes back.

And then the dam breaks. Big, meaty, juicy, salty tears fall from my eyes and into my wild boar ragù. Head in hands, I sob quietly, alone in an empty restaurant, while the waiter looks askance. Then the tears strangely morph into something else, and I laugh hysterically at my absolute, complete, total and utter ridiculousness. God save me from ever taking myself too seriously. And then, sense of humour restored, I allow myself a little bit of pride. Travel ain't easy, whatever the rewards. I eat a few more scoops of my now extra salty gnocchi, and head back to the hotel for bed. Sorry Pisa, but sometimes you just have to write a day off.

Maybe it was the thunderstorm of tears that cleared the air, but I wake the next day feeling remarkably human. The antibiotics seem to be finally kicking in, and I'm excited to get my, ahem, teeth stuck into Pisa. Truth be told, I've not been at my best since I landed in Skopje, and I've been trying to pretend everything is OK. Have I finally turned a corner? I hope so. Still sans satnav I attempt to navigate myself across the river and through the side streets of Pisa to climb the famous Leaning Tower. I'm using a tourist map and good old fashioned common sense, so naturally I arrive 20 minutes late for my noon appointment.

If you read anything about Pisa online you will probably notice that it gets rather damned with faint praise. If Tuscany was Destiny's Child, then Pisa would be Michelle Williams to Florence's Beyoncé and Lecce's Kelly Rowland. That's unfortunate company to keep, although personally I always preferred Williams' smoky, under-used vocal chops. If Pisa was in Ohio, or Bedfordshire, or actually most other regions of the world, it would be the prettiest gal in town. But all it really gets is 'Well it ain't Florence, is it?' Well no it ain't. But have you ever tried to get a taxi out of Florence after 6 p.m.? I thought I was gonna have to sleep rough last time I was there.

Pisa is pretty rather than beautiful. It doesn't come at you tap-dancing with a Carmen Miranda fruit hat on its head, a whole bunch of break-dancing elephants as back-up singing *Life is a Cabaret*, like Florence/Beyoncé does. It skips up to you, curtsies, and sweetly blows you a kiss. Obviously, mostly you'd want the former, but there's a time and a place for the latter, and recovering from oral trauma is one of them.

When I finally glimpse the tower in the flesh, so to speak, I do what everybody must do. I laugh. It's actually really, really funny, in the best, most childish way possible. Yes, I know there are serious architectural issues to be talked about here, but amid the symmetry and occasional pomposity of Pisa's other, non-leaning buildings, it's full-on comedy. It's as if it's photobombing the rest of the buildings as they stand there looking all serious and self-important, shouting 'Woo-hoo! Look at me!' I don't actually buy the subsidence theory. I think it's just a renaissance building with a refreshingly childish sense of humour. Almost as funny are the hundreds of Koreans standing on walls doing the 'Ooh, I'm holding it up' or 'Whoops it fell on my head' pose. If you ignore the tower and photograph them from the opposite direction all you have is scores of voguing Koreans on walls, which is never a bad thing.

In my 1970s childhood, the Leaning Tower of Pisa (which we used to hilariously rename Pizza) was, alongside Manuel from *Fawlty Towers*, the pre-eminent symbol of European dopey ridiculousness among British schoolchildren. I find the Tower utterly charming and I think if we could do something similar with Big Ben it might cheer us all up a bit and stop us taking ourselves so bloody seriously.

Because I'm late, my ticket has gone missing and I'm directed to about four different offices before I can ascend the tower. I'm fairly sanguine about the whole thing because I reckon, correctly, that the view is definitely better from downstairs but much hand waving ensues from all involved. Excuse me for my crude cultural stereotypes, but Italians do love to make a drama out of a crisis. They're nuts, basically. But none the worse for it.

I meander back through Pisa and stop at a little outdoor café, where I am served perfect, soft tagliatelle carbonara by a man with nasal hair so long, luscious and thick I could have swung from it, Tarzan-like, shouting 'Wheeeee!' I do wonder why nobody had ever thought to drop a nasal hair clipper in his Christmas stocking. They're cheap from Poundland you know. A pound, actually. His nasal tresses have such a lovely sheen I suspect he maybe even conditions them. The pain is at the lowest ebb it has been for days and I'm actually feeling a kind of peaceful euphoria. It's a perfect moment, like that brief moment of utter bliss you feel after you throw up, when you have food poisoning. Then a really scary clown statue person jumps in my face demanding euros. He sees the utter terror in my eyes.

As always happens when I come to Italy, as I walk back to my hotel I begin to accept its oddness, forgive its absolute and utter refusal to make any attempts to join the rest of us in the 21st century, and remember that, rather like a particularly tricky diva, Italy can afford to be like that because it is Italy. And yes, Italians, who incidentally know everything about everything, *are* correct. It is, with its shitty Wi-Fi, lack of ATMs and toilets, and refusal to take credit cards (I can't *begin* to imagine what that's all about) still undoubtedly one of the greatest travel experiences in the world. It makes no attempt whatsoever to fall over backwards for tourists. Accept it on its terms, or don't accept it at all. Italia isn't fussed. It's incorrigible and of course, probably for that very reason, I love it. Like Italian men, I love it, but I wouldn't marry it.

There's a grand and shiny launderette around the corner from my hotel, so having been on the road with a severely depleted supply of clothes and underwear, I take the opportunity to wash everything I've used. There is a real life Nick Kamen in there washing his smalls and he explains to me in perfect English how to use the machines. This is rare. Most Italians don't bother to speak foreign languages, and fair play to them for that. He is as beautiful as a Michelangelo statue. He reminds me that many times through my trip to Pisa I've thought to myself, 'Wow, isn't this a gay friendly city!' by virtue of the number of pretty lesbian couples I see smooching around town. Then I take a second glance and realise that one of the Italian lesbians is actually a teenage Italian boy with shoulder length hair, full lips and long dark lashes. Which begs the question – do teenage Italian boys look like pretty lesbians or do pretty lesbians look like teenage Italian boys? I do like to debate the great philosophical issues of our day; I think Italy brings this out in me.

Dinner ensues, and more pasta, this time *orecchiette* (little ears: my absolute new favourite) with grated courgette, prawns, garlic, parsley, and lots and lots of cream and salty butter. Oh. My. Word. Yes Italy, I know you don't need my forgiveness, but regardless, I forgive you everything, my child.

That night I take a taxi to Pisa's one and only men's bar. And no, it's not a sporting club. You may have noticed, I very slyly, subtly and surreptitiously 'came out' to you in the last couple of paragraphs. I know, absolutely seamless wasn't it? I wasn't sure, when I started writing this, whether I would, but it's kind of untenable that I don't.

I'm not massively struck on self-revelatory journalism, but at the same time, I feel a bit of a dick travelling around Europe and passing judgement on everything without giving any clue to who I am. And this is me. So there you go. (Awkward pause.) It's done. Hopefully we can all move on and find a new understanding.

Anyway, the other thing you don't know about me is that I'm catnip to Italians. Don't ask me why. I'm invisible to Iberians, boring to Bretons, not pertinent to Nova Scotians, trivial to Transylvanians, uninteresting to Uzbeks, worthless to Walloons and largely irrelevant to people from the Ivory Coast. But Italians fucking love me. And that ain't a bad deal, if you had to pick one out of the atlas of hot international homosexualists. I'd certainly swap 'em for Finns. So I go to a bar, I meet a man called Gianluca, and for a couple of hours I largely forget that my wisdom teeth exist. Charmingly, he gives me his number and asks for me to stay in touch. Sheesh, I'm hot. Readers, I've lost it, though, you know. I imagine he's still tearfully searching the streets of Pisa looking for his lost English love. Gianni, if you're reading this, get in touch...

COMPARING THE COMPARERS

I'll nail my colours to the mast right away. In the world of flight metasearch engines, it can be confusing knowing who you can trust. Some seem to have information that others do not; others work better than their rivals occasionally, and yet other times perform miserably. You can lose days shaving a few quid off a flight. There is an all-pervasive sense that we can do better than what we have been offered. And all of this benefits the airlines. They want us to be aware of their cheap flights. But they don't want to make it too easy. Then nobody would pay top dollar.

I've tested our search engines with three routes from London leaving on the same date, 25th January: London to Edinburgh, London to Budapest, and London to Tbilisi in Georgia, return, with one change en route. Prices have been rounded up and down to the nearest pound.

ADIOSO

I like Adioso. I want to love it. It so nearly 'gets' the importance of flexibility when you're searching for flights, but then it misses by a mile.

Adioso promises similar flexibility to Kiwi.com, and its array of destinations is incredible. You can search North America, 'the Americas', or even ethno-linguistic categories such as Latin America, subjective categories such as 'most romantic' and even defunct nations (though maybe not for long if Putin gets his way) such as the USSR. The trouble is you are still restricted to one outgoing city, which means a lot of back and forth. Kiwi.com assumes I'm not afraid to hop between destinations, but Adioso still mostly assumes we want to travel in a straight line and back. Using its delightful vagueness, I ask it to find me return flights to the Baltic States, sometime in February, for about a week. It finds me a 16-day return for £89. A quick hop on Kiwi.com easily finds me a 14-day return for £63.50.

Something tells me Adioso could still become the best search engine we have ever seen, its heart is certainly in the right place, but at the moment it's best for playing around with and finding unusual cheap destinations, then bagging the flights for less money on Skyscanner and Kiwi.com. Every so often it does come up with some incredible bargains but its success rate is haphazard. If you have the time or the inclination it can be a useful addition.

London to Edinburgh	£102
London to Tbilisi	£231 *changing at Istanbul, via Cheapoair
London to Budapest	£24

CHEAPFLIGHTSFINDER

In theory, this website should do in an instant what I'm trying to do in this chapter. Cheapflightsfinder attempts to run your flight requirements through most of the best travel meta search engines, including the likes of Kiwi.com, Momondo and Kayak. This, though, it fails to do on my iPad, operating with a clunky and slow interface. Frankly, in my experience, it would be quicker to search each site individually yourself.

GOOGLE FLIGHTS SEARCH

What you would imagine to be the daddy of all search engines predictably offers a smooth searching experience but, oddly given its clout, is way behind the competition when it comes to price and flexibility. Unfortunately, it's a big fat fail for Google.

London to Edinburgh	£117
London to Tbilisi	£220 *changing at Istanbul
London to Budapest	£20

HIPMUNK

Scoring high on cuteness but low on flexibility, Hipmunk claims to have the best selection, and boasts of how it's easy to use to compare prices. It is easy to use but probably because it doesn't do much. This is a rigid search engine, which will offer little to the adventurous for who needs his or her imagination sparking. Annoyingly, although it's also a portal to other sites, you have to run your search all over again once you are connected to, say, Ryanair. Frankly if I was looking to be impressed by moving cartoon animals, I'd stick on Tom and Jerry.

London to Edinburgh	£117
London to Tbilisi	£247 *changing at Kiev, via Travelocity
London to Budapes	£21

MOMONDO

More of the same from Momondo which again is an uninventive search engine other than it deigns to divide its results into three categories of cheapest, quickest, and the spurious 'best'. I'll be the judge of that, thanks, Momondo.

London to Edinburgh   £86

London to Tbilisi   £211 *changing at Istanbul

London to Budapest   £20

KAYAK

Allows a few days' flexibility on your bookings; I couldn't get the Kayak mobile site to work at all on my iPad. The site recognises the advantages of booking only outward-bound flights, calling these 'hacker fares'.

London to Edinburgh   £76

London to Tbilisi   £218 *changing at Istanbul, via Kiwi.com

London to Budapest   £20 (directed through Ryanair site)

SKYSCANNER

When you become used to the simplicity of using Skyscanner to find out, for instance, the cost of a flight to Warsaw for a week, it's hard to imagine going back. Skyscanner's ridiculously simple yet clever interface finds you the cheapest flights on a chosen day, month or year. Instead of having to hop between rival sites, and different dates or departure or arrival cities, Skyscanner was the site which provided me with the travel epiphany which led to this book being written. Since then Skyscanner has just continued with the innovations, and it only links you to the booking site, without taking a commission, which makes this incredibly rewarding website as close as there is to an act of love in the online capitalist world.

London to Edinburgh   £74

London to Tbilisi   £224 *changing at Istanbul

London to Budapest   £20

KIWI.COM (FORMERLY SKYPICKER)

Unlike Skyscanner, Kiwi.com charges a (teeny) commission fee, but we'll forgive them that. After all, a couple of percent on a three quid flight is next to nothing. Kiwi.com basically took the Skyscanner model but razzed it up a bit and made it even more flexible and thrilling. Not to say I prefer it – that would be like picking between the ABBA girls. And. I. Will. Never. Do. That. They also made it even more intelligent and user friendly. It's easier on Kiwi.com to search over a range of dates, but perhaps even better than that, it will also search for cheap flights that aren't direct. So, as long as your outward or return journey is less than 75 hours or so, it will dig out massively cheap routes you probably never dreamed of to the US, Europe or beyond.

Now, I don't know about you, but a flight to the US which includes a 12-hour layover in, say, Reykjavik, sounds like a pain in the arse. But Kiwi.com digs up some unexpected routes you may have never considered which are cheap as chips. So the same trip to America, with a two-night stop in Iceland, which can constitute part of the holiday rather than an annoying layover – well, now you're talking. Kiwi.com automatically has access to the myriad connections and complications of the international flight route database, enabling you to thread together your own personalised itinerary.

London to Edinburgh £86

London to Tbilisi   £194, *changing at Istanbul

London to Budapest £18

So it's clear that Skyscanner and Kiwi.com are the greatest flight search engines out there on price. But these prices don't tell the whole story, however. What Skyscanner and Kiwi.com also allow you to do is to play around with departure and arrival dates, connecting cities and unusual routes, so that you can reduce your costs and widen your holiday options massively. The others are, comparatively, as flexible as concrete...

CHAPTER 5

TROUBLE IN PARADISE

I feel my whole body de-stress just stepping on to the tarmac at Thessaloniki airport. It's mid October but the sun shines brightly and the warmth wraps around my bones. Just knowing I'm in Greece makes me happy. I've been only a handful of times, but there's something about this place that always leaves me with a warm, fuzzy feeling. You are accepted into this country not just as a tourist, not just as a guest, but like family.

It makes me cry when I see how Greece is being abused by stupid people who know the price of everything but the value of nothing. When you come here, and you see how people help each other through whichever pickle they are facing, you wonder if maybe we are the unfortunate ones. In London, the completely unregulated housing market is creating a situation surely as dangerous and destructive as what is happening here in the southern Balkans. Families who have lived in communities for generations, even the well paid middle classes, are being driven out of their homes because of rental increases above 25 per cent a year. But because the Greek budgetary problems have been labelled a 'crisis', this city has a problem and apparently Britain does not. I don't see it that way. The same untethered capitalism which many here believe is destroying their communities is doing the same thing back home, and nobody even seems to have noticed. When will *we* be permitted to call it a crisis? I digress. Thessaloniki is a peach of a city, the most important port of the northern Aegean. And yes, guess what? I'm back in Macedonia. I've flown 1,700 miles to get back to more or less where I started. Thessaloniki is just 150 miles from Skopje, though culturally it's a different world. It cost me just £48 for three flights to bring me back to Macedonia. The cheapest local flight, via Istanbul, would set me back £128. There are no direct flights at all between two of the three Macedonias. (Bulgaria has Pirin Macedonia as well.) Perhaps it might be a good idea to get a flight going between these two estranged cousins. The lack of contact seems to have added to a complete lack of mutual understanding and trust. And yet in reality, Skopje and Thessaloniki, even if they are on different cultural poles, have so much more in common than what drives them apart.

Thessaloniki doesn't *feel* like a Greek city, and – whisper it around here because they probably don't know this – just over 100 years ago it very much wasn't. In 1890, only 13.5 per cent of the population here were Greek, while 46 per cent were Jewish and 22 per cent Muslim, mainly of Turkish origin. By the eve of World War I, the Greek population of Salonika, as it was then known, was a quarter, still much less than the Muslim population of 29 per cent and the Jewish community of 39 per cent, not to mention a sizeable Bulgarian population. With its wide boulevards and grand squares, Gothic and Baroque remnants and smoky café culture, it reminds me more of an elegant, southerly, nautical Budapest than noisy, squawking Athens. It only latterly strikes me that this is surely the legacy of one of the Mediterranean's biggest and most successful Jewish communities. Though they are mostly long gone, murdered by Nazis, their presence is still very much felt.

This was a multi-cultural city, where the footprints of the Byzantine and Ottoman empires can still be seen in layers and layers of architecture. But Balkan wars followed by two World Wars devastated this doughty Aegean matron. The bitter Balkan conflagration, a rehearsal for World War I, saw the departure of the Slavic population and thousands of Muslims, Turkish or otherwise, when the city was won by Greece. The wars of the early twentieth century saw the city overwhelmed when tens of thousands of Greek refugees arrived from Asia Minor and Bulgaria. In 1917, the Great Fire devastated huge swathes of a city already on its knees. Next came the disaster of the Greco-Turkish war of 1919–1922, where the Greek Prime Minister Venizelos, egged on by British Prime Minister Lloyd George, undertook to conquer great swathes of Asia Minor around the Black Sea and the Greek dominated city of Smyrna. Reinvigorated by Atatürk, the Turks came roaring back, full of fury and vengeance. Hundreds of thousands of civilians from both communities were slaughtered and beautiful cosmopolitan Smyrna, in 1922, was wiped from the face of the earth and concreted over as Izmir, just as polyglot Salonika was renamed Greek Thessaloniki. According to the Treaty of Lausanne, a pragmatic but horrible solution was found, with the remaining Greeks thrown out of Asia Minor, while the Greek Muslims were slung across the Aegean to Turkey. Communities of old friends, who had lived in peace, were torn apart and history in both countries largely rewritten to imply that the cities and towns around the Aegean and Black Sea basin had always been either Greek or Turkish.

Forgive me when I jump between this city's two monikers, I prefer Salonika because it is neither Greek, nor Turk, nor Bulgarian… but international. Like Smyrna, these are the names of worlds lost, like Atlantis. But how much prettier do Salonika and Smyrna sound, than Thessaloniki and Izmir…?

The remaining Muslims were deported from Salonika to live in the former homes of the Greeks in Smyrna, who in turn were squeezed into the properties of the evicted Salonikan Muslims. It was a brutal ending to centuries of living side-by-side – followed by the destruction of one of Europe's oldest Jewish communities in World War II, slaughtered en masse after the city was strafed by the Luftwaffe. Thessaloniki suffered utter horror for more than half a century. The miracle is that this now feels like such a happy, positive place. You sense that after the century that went before, not even Angela Merkel could kill Thessaloniki's collective spirit.

Despite its ancient past, Thessaloniki feels like a very young city. This is a university town, and the past perhaps taught its people to live for the day. The Greeks are the Geordies of the Mediterranean, sentimental, party loving and family orientated. This is unequivocally Greece's second city, and one of the most important ports in the Mediterranean still – yet it barely registers in popular consciousness in Britain or the USA. Corfu, Crete, Rhodes and Mykonos: apart from Athens, all we ever pay attention to is Greece's sublime island life. But Thessaloniki offers a richer Greek experience with cool bars and sexy food. It has that bracing optimism and never-say-die spirit of all great port cities. All roads lead down to the sea, where you can find a nice sundowner shack, drink ouzo and eat fresher-than-fresh calamari, and feel that sense of peace and completeness which a sea view always brings. With a population of around 370,000, a thriving arts scene and perhaps the best party circuit anywhere in Greece (forget Kavos or Faliraki, this is the real deal), not to mention a year-round mellow climate, virtually no crime, and the nicest, most welcoming people you are likely to find anywhere on the continent – I really can't think of a better low-cost flight destination. Prices are keen, for everything from taxis to food. The one exception, oddly, is drinks, whether they be soft or hard, but stick to the local stuff and you'll save a packet.

My first meal is the one and only Greek *gyros* at Devido, the city's premier purveyor of juicy, grilled, marinated meats where the counter heaves with salads, sauces and tender barbecue delicacies. This is fast food the way it ought to be done, and proof that done well, it doesn't have to make our kids obese. The Greek *gyros* and *souvlaki* are tainted by association with the greasy British doner kebab, loaded with things you would hesitate to feed to your dog. The *gyros* is a masterpiece of Greek genius: marinated grilled and charcoaled pork, chicken and lamb, crisp, heavenly salads, preferably featuring feta, hummus, tzatziki and at this restaurant a smoked paprika '*sos*' plus smoky aubergine dip, chips of course and all wrapped up in fresh baked bread. You'll see low quality versions of *gyros* and *souvlaki* near tourist fleshpots on the holiday islands. But the real deal, the places the Greeks go to, are as important a part of national culture as brandy, the acropolis and hating Angela Merkel. It's a defining part of food heritage every bit as delicious as fish and chips, paella or pizza. I pray for the day *gyros* takes off in Britain and the horrendous late night doner disappears forever.

After lunch I visit the Municipal Art Gallery, a beautiful example of eclecticist architecture with a tragic history in the heart of the city. It was built in the early 20th century, when Thessaloniki was still ruled by the Ottomans, by Dino Fernandez Diaz, an industrialist of Italian-Jewish heritage. The villa was passed to his daughter Alina where she lived with her Christian, lower-class husband against the will of her family. When the Nazis took Salonika in 1941, they confiscated the property. Sensing the impending slaughter of Salonika's Jews, the family fled to Italy, but following that country's takeover by the Nazis, most were captured and murdered by the SS – Alina and her husband survived. The mansion itself is not a sad place, however, but strangely optimistic; the windows are big and generous, light flooding in everywhere and warmth seeping from every crevice, perhaps reflecting the forbidden love affair which triumphed here over prejudice, long before madness and savagery took over. The art, at the time I visit a collection of works by Greek Australians, is modern, upbeat... happy. What you imagine Alina would have liked.

I've got a room at The Met down by the docks; a vision in dark wood and brown velvet, it's a shamelessly hip hotel, which seems a little incongruous amid the timelessness of Salonika. But it's a cosy, relaxing space and a nice place for an early evening drink before you head off to party central. The best thing about the hotel is its restaurant, Chan, which does a nifty riff on Chinese–Greek fusion cuisine, which is a much more harmonious blend of ingredients and cooking styles than you might imagine. The restaurant is sexy dark, especially if you're looking a bit rough, but maybe not so great if, like me, you suffer from poor night vision and run the risk of blundering face first into your partner's chocolate bombe. It's all quite blackly sensuous, the kinda place you'd expect to see Batman playing footsie with Catwoman over the crispy duck and the massive golden chocolate balls with butter caramel. With a rooftop pool and bar, featuring DJs and amazing views over the city and out to sea as far as Mount Olympus, this is definitely a place where money is no object and hedonism rules. It's good to see that's still the case in Hellas, but whisper it quietly lest Frau Merkel comes and takes ownership of your side order of truffle fries. Over dinner with a Greek friend I met travelling and her beautiful aunt and uncle we ponder how 65 years spent trying to recover some sort of German national reputation following World War II has been squandered in 12 months by the German government's handling of the Greeks.

Talk of a 'Greek bailout', it strikes me, is an absolute red herring. The real bailout is of the German and French banks which irresponsibly and greedily lent money to a country which was not able to pay that money back. If Greece defaulted, those banks would face collapse. So let's get it right, folks: European money is being used to prop up Franco-German money speculators, not to help Greek people who have been offered no long-term way out of penury.

When I mention the European Union to my Greek friend, angry tears fill her eyes.

'What "union" is this, of which you talk?' she demands. 'What family cuts the hands and feet off one of its children, then tells it to work harder?'

We leave the restaurant and jump in the hotel's free shuttle to the city centre. It's fortunate that Greece does a nice line in black humour, but I'm not convinced Japanese visitors would be hugely amused by the title of the city's pre-eminent gay bar, Enola. It's a funny, irreverent place which lays on a nice spread in eight-foot trannies sporting psychopath chic. You're guaranteed a good laugh here, and to leave behind your problems for another day. The welcome is as warm as moussaka and I note that Greek young clubbers don't have the same glazed, drugged up expression of London clubbers, gay or straight. Are we absolutely *sure* we have identified the correct city in crisis?

Travelling with no bags in the hold, you really have to pare down the liquids you bring with you on a month-long journey around Europe. I miss the feeling of elegance my Dior Homme brings me, even when I look as rough as a bag of dead ferrets. I can live without my little luxuries, but in Greece, I *really* miss my Grecian 2000. My hair at 23 was thick and luscious, hanging in a very fetching and fashionable (at the time) man-bob around my ears. Time has sapped the pigment and thinned its lustre. It's wispy and salt and pepper now. OK, with the emphasis on salt. It never bothered me before but in Greece I mourn my lost youth, and all the time I threw away worrying that I looked horrendous. I didn't. But if you are over 35 you will know what I mean. As they say correctly, youth is wasted on the young. The Greeks are a handsome bunch by any mark, male or female. But in Thessaloniki I feel seriously deprived by the men of all ages with hair and eyelashes as thick and black as treacle. Poor Telly 'Kojak' Savalas. No wonder he moved to America. And now I know why they call it *Grecian* 2000.

Here is a piece of information for those of you worrying about getting older and nobody wanting you. When you are of optimum height, age, hair colour and body size, you fall into the 'general interest' category, which means that you are generally acceptable to the majority of the population, although obviously the competition is fierce. Once you fall outside this category, you become of 'specialist interest', which means that while 95 per cent of people would rather go for the conventional norm, 5 per cent go fucking crazy for you and literally can't get enough of you. You become a fetish if you like. I know a woman in Leytonstone who is 35 stone, give or take a few bags of potatoes, and she gets more male attention than you can shake a stick at, dogging up at Hollow Ponds. I'm like heroin to the part of the world population which likes greying Geordies about a stone over their optimum weight. It's a niche, I grant you, but I consequently do better than I did when I was young and pretty and of general interest. Why does no one tell you that when you are fretting over your first grey hairs or turning 25? So yeah, despite my lack of lustrous locks, I am grateful to attract a little attention.

At the bar, as gay and straight boys and girls dance and drink and carouse and flirt and snog and party in the happiest, most attitude-free environment you could hope to encounter, I notice an extraordinary thing, something I can't imagine seeing in any other major European city. Along the bar next to where I'm dancing, there are about seven wallets and five mobile phones. Their owners have just plonked them down and wandered off to boogie or gossip with their mates. Were I that bad, or that desperate, I could have snaffled the lot in a jiffy. Remember, this is a country where people are, apparently, down to their last few euros.

Yet nobody steals off their neighbour. The Greek people have been smeared by many slanders since the Eurozone crisis kicked off, but the notion that Greece cooked the books to get in the euro, and that somehow Greek people are therefore less honest than their northern neighbours, seems to me the most wicked lie of all. I lived in a part of Manchester where society had broken down so much that people would burgle their next door neighbours. That's unthinkable here. If Greek politicians did indeed 'cook the books' then I suggest that the German government, now such a stickler for financial clarity, was happy not to look too closely as it drove through its scheme for a common currency. Before the euro, Germany couldn't export a pint of milk to Austria, such was the strength of the Deutschmark. Now you can buy cheap German and northern European yoghurts in Greece. Who the hell would buy watery, limp German, Dutch or British yoghurt in Greece, where this homemade delicacy is as thick, silky and lustrous as the local men's hair? Sorry, I'm dancing in a bar in a fantastically fun Greek city and I'm talking politics. But you are never far from politics in this land right now. So here are the facts. In 2014, Germany's trade surplus was $250 billion, or 7 per cent of GDP. That continues an unending upward trend that's been happening since 2000. Not at all coincidentally, the euro was launched in non-physical form in January 1999. All participating countries had their currencies locked together from that point. The euro is too weak to reflect the economies of northern Europe, and too strong to reflect the economies of southern Europe and Ireland. In this context, it is sickening to hear of northern Europe 'bailing out' the south. Greece and others fell victim to a massive financial scam driven by Germany. They should be suing for compensation and ditching the euro as quickly as possible. It would be interesting to see how quickly Angela Merkel came to the negotiating table then. It's interesting that Poland, which stayed out of the single currency, is the best performing economy of the new accession states in east/central Europe. It would do well to stick to its guns and to the zloty. In the meantime, Germany, a country which plundered and committed mass murder in Greece within living memory, has taken ownership of Greek airports as compensation. Does that not strike you as sinister?

Lunch the next day is at the charming, nautically themed Xontro Alati, right next to the city's buzzing food market. There are international restaurants in Thessaloniki but why would you bother when this city showcases the best regional Greek food from all over the mainland and islands. Order piscine treats here: the fish soup with saffron, served in a massive bowl, will gladden the heart and soothe the soul of the weariest traveller. With my mouth more or less fixed, I decide to take on the challenge of attempting to get my phone to remember it is a mobile phone. My kind and funny friend Klelia, at Thessaloniki Tourism, offers to let me contact Virgin Media from her office phone. Remember, this is the same Virgin Media which cheerily advises you to give them a call if your mobile phone is broken. Hmmm. I will try to avoid going into intricate detail of the four hours of my trip I utterly wasted pleading with my mobile phone provider to get me a working mobile phone. But here are the highlights…

When you call Virgin to report a problem with your phone, you are initially transferred to a call centre in the Philippines staffed by girls who sound like they are still in junior high, and issue the kind of 'Gee! Have a nice day!' inanities which would render an interview with Britney Spears like an audience with Stephen Fry. No matter how deep your frustration, how epic your unhappiness with their service, no matter how gnashing your teeth are, these sweet girls will reply in the manner of an American burger shop automaton, straight off a script, in a perky tone which ought to be reserved for saying, 'And would sir like fries with that?' They would make world class babysitters but know absolutely nothing about mobile phones. As I write this, I am already contemplating lying down in a dark room for an hour and meditating because I am due another phone call to Virgin after which I always have a little cry. I do wonder whether Richard Branson keeps these poor young ladies in cages in Manila feeding them sugar, Xanax, Adderal, Coco Pops, Ritalin, Love Hearts, Steps' *Greatest Hits*, more sugar and Prozac. If you phoned up and told them that two of your triplets had been stolen and eaten by wolves, they would surely reply, 'Oh dear. And did sir have a good weekend?' But it's just a process you have to go through before you speak to anyone at Virgin who may actually know something about something. I genuinely, genuinely believe that it has been created to make sure customers give up the will to live before they have a chance to put forward their enquiry or complaint. The Manila call centre ladies should be locked in a room with depressed Balkan lounge cover version singers, in the hope that some kind of equilibrium might actually be found.

I explain the nature of my distress in some detail to the hyper-ventilatingly happy Stacey at the end of the phone, trying not to grind my teeth.

'Well thank you sir, and did sir have an enjoyable and happy weekend?'

'No, it was absolutely bloody horrible,' I reply. 'I have spent ten hours online trying to find ways to contact Virgin Media because the best advice you can give to someone with a phone which *you* broke with a faulty software download that makes it forget it's a phone is to give them a ring. I am completely unable to do the work I came to Europe to do. You have screwed up my satnav so I have to spend fortunes on taxis and don't know my way around the streets of an unknown European city. And I'm cut off from the people I love. So no, I have had a horrible weekend and it's entirely your fault. Since you ask.' This response was clearly not included in Stacey's two-hour training programme and she throws me back to the London technical department with the speed with which one passes a shitting, nappyless newborn back to its mother. Of course I don't actually personally blame the person on the other side of the phone; I take care to keep my voice low, even at moments of high provocation and frustration. I think I manage not to swear. But it's incredibly hard. Having gone through the rigmarole of getting passed from the high-pitched call centre zombies of Manila, I explain my woes to someone in their technical team in London, and just as we are making some kind of progress, I am cut off. I then have to restart the process from scratch, including all the associated menus and recorded messages, plus of course my friends in Manila. This happens, I think, five times. Now I'm typing through gritted teeth. Often the moment of disconnection seems to happen when it dawns on the person at the other end of the phone that this is not a simple problem to solve. Coincidence? Who knows!

We ascertain that my phone no longer recognises itself as a phone and that this is probably due to an error with the new system software. We reinstall the software using a PC to no avail. I'm advised to reset my phone from scratch. I'm desperate so I do it. I lose heaps of important data, but my phone is still no longer a phone. I tell them they need to provide me with a working mobile phone seeing as they broke my last one. They say that if I return it to them they will fix it for when I get back. I explain that for me to do my job, and stay sane and safe I need a working mobile phone now. And that I need to keep this one until it arrives because in the meantime at least it works with Wi-Fi. Not possible, they say. We go round and round in circles. My friend is becoming concerned about the four hours I have spent on the phone to England. So am I.

'It's quite simple,' I tell them. 'I pay for you to provide me with a working mobile phone. You broke my mobile phone. Do what I pay you for.'

The last guy is bullish to say the least. 'We are only obliged to provide you with a working mobile phone while you are in the UK,' he tells me. 'Your contract says nothing about taking it abroad.'

'Ooh! You don't put that in your advertising, do you?' I tell him, kind of disgusted while feeling refreshed that someone has finally said something true. 'I have been on this phone for four hours,' I tell him. 'Can you *please* give me an email address so we can continue this conversation?'

'I can't give you an email address.' Virgin staff are very adept at using the word *can't* when they actually mean the word *won't*.

'Yes you can,' I say.

'I can't.'

'You mean you won't.'

'I can't.'

'Why?'

'Because we don't have them.'

Now I start to laugh. 'Yes you *do*!'

'We *don't.*'

'Mate, you *do*. Please don't tell me porkie pies. Of course you do.' I'm laughing hysterically now and half crying at the same time.

'No we don't.' He is firm about this.

'So you are a company named Virgin *Media* which has no email? Do you use carrier pigeons?'

'We have no outside email.'

Now I'm really laughing. He's not finding my hilarity hilarious. 'Mate, I'm in Wonderland. After four hours Virgin Media tell me they are a company with no outside email. I feel like Alice. I've fallen down the rabbit hole. Are you Tweedle Dee or...' Certainly their boss could do a nice turn as an idiotic, grinning Cheshire Cat. After four hours of calling on a beautiful, sunny day in northern Greece, I have achieved nothing more than a minor nervous breakdown to show for my hard slog. My friend urges me to pull the journalist card. It's not something I'm keen to do, ever, because it's so bloody naff, but what the heck, I'm desperate. 'I need you to know that I am writing about this for a book and several features,' I say.

'Don't threaten me,' comes the reply.

'Whoooah! Steady on there, cowboy. Don't you think that if I was trying to threaten you I would have done this four hours ago when the glorious Greek autumn afternoon was but young?' I say. 'Aren't you embarrassed?' I ask him. 'I mean, seriously, it must be awful for you having to peddle this absolute nonsense to people crying down the phone on a daily basis?'

'I'm not embarrassed at all,' he tells me. 'I used to work for T-Mobile and Vodafone and they're much worse,' he tells me proudly. Jeez, how bad can they be, I wonder? Do they actually come around to your house and rape your cat? At the time of writing I have still not sorted out this mess, despite having paid out a few more hundred quid to Richard Branson, who is apparently engaged currently in a space tourism project which intends to send Victoria Principal and Angelina Jolie to the moon. Or summink. I earnestly wish he would stick to the day job and provide me with the working mobile phone I have paid him more than fairly for. A working mobile phone is a must on a trip like this.

I think I need to set up a Virgin survivors' group therapy meeting very soon. But my advice to you is take a good mobile phone with you if you are going away for a bit, and if you can find or borrow one take a spare in case some eejit download breaks it for you. I feel bad moaning about this. First world problems, right? I *am* aware Virgin Media are not quite the Khmer Rouge. But they spread unhappiness and take money for things they don't actually supply. Collectively centuries of life and human peace of mind are lost in the Virgin call centre labyrinth.

The next day, recovered from my phone ordeal, I'm taken on a tour of Salonika Old Town, up in the hills above the city, walking along the old city walls which have seen invasion after invasion but now gaze dreamily and peacefully over the bay shimmering in the Sunday morning sunshine. This was where the first refugees, forced out of Asia Minor, arrived and were squeezed into the homes of departed Turks and Bulgarians. It is the most architecturally complete section of this often disjointed city. A city where perhaps there has been a reluctance to preserve parts of the past. Because that, the Greeks fear, might remind the world that this was, not so long ago, an international city belonging to no nation.

There is a lot of graffiti in Thessaloniki, some of it witty or funny, such as the proclamation to 'blow up your granny' in party district; some just destructive, on historic buildings which don't deserve to be defaced. I wonder, to my tour guide, whether there is a disconnection between young people and Thessaloniki's former life as Salonika.

'I don't think there has been much honesty in the teaching of the past either here or in Turkey. But it is time,' she says. Elina has been involved in cultural exchange programmes with Izmir, Thessaloniki's sister in suffering. Just as Thessaloniki was Salonika, Izmir was Smyrna, the greatest Greek city in the world – far bigger and more successful than Athens on the eve of its utter destruction. Much of what we now think of as Thessaloniki – the food, the culture, the traditions – is actually Smyrniot, and much of Izmir is old Salonika, as the two cities exchanged their unwanted residents and erased their collective memories. It seems to me terribly sad and I wish I could somehow visit these lost cities. A cultural bridgehead and reconciliation between Thessaloniki and Izmir would be a start.

'And why not a council of the Balkans?' I ask, where Greeks, Turks, Albanians, Macedonians, Bulgarians, Serbs and others could try to work together.

'It would be chaos,' she laughs wryly. 'They would kill each other!' She is one of the few people I have met anywhere in the Balkans, Greece, Macedonia, Croatia, and Montenegro, who is able to speak from an international perspective. Most people around these parts are the most incredibly kind and hospitable folk you will meet anywhere in the world. They will take you in their homes, treat you like family, give you their last meal. But mention their neighbours and they spit out racist opinions that would make a UKipper blush. Otherwise perfectly cosmopolitan, successful people. One of the people I meet on my travels in Thessaloniki, a very sophisticated and otherwise intelligent person, tells me she has met people from Skopje and they are fundamentally dishonest. I mean goodness gracious. Separation of peoples around here may have preserved peace but it has created demons next door.

I love Greece. It feels like paradise, for many reasons, not least its unmatched genuine warmth and kindness. But I feel embarrassment that they have done so much to block their neighbours in Macedonian Macedonia from a place of safety in the EU and NATO. It's like finding out a much loved family member is a spiteful racist. Frankly it shames this beautiful country and I hope it comes to its senses before another tragedy visits the Balkans, one which will cause havoc for Greece too.

Down at beautiful Agia Sofia, we see Russian and Bulgarian tourists arriving to pray. Despite the destruction, this place is still redolent with some of the atmosphere of the old Balkans, of Byzantines and Ottomans. The place, modelled on Istanbul/ Constantinople's Hagia Sofia, has changed from church to mosque just as Thessaloniki has changed identities throughout its history. Lunch is taken at the graceful and engaging Myrsini, near the city's ancient White Tower, the best Cretan restaurant in town. This is no small boast, given that most Greeks rate Crete's culinary delicacies as the best the nation has to offer. Order the chef's specials or the famous Cretan rabbit. The massive lamb meatballs in tomato and oregano were possibly better even than the best *albondigas* I've eaten in Spain. This place is famous for its raki, and their '*Rakomeze*' includes raki plus six tapas-sized dishes for six euros. Incredible food at an amazing price. My last afternoon is spent mooching along the bay with my sweet and gentle Klelia, picking at seafood and pickles and looking out across the Aegean towards Turkey, over moody seas where countless refugees have drowned escaping Syria and the latest brutal population expulsions in this part of the world. Thessaloniki has seen it too many times. If this city had any money, wouldn't it make a great home for those desperate Syrian Christians and Muslims, with their shared Ottoman past and culture which is far closer than anybody around these parts seems to admit. It certainly seems to make a lot more sense to find them homes here than sending them off to remote Scottish islands. Couldn't the rest of Europe pay Greece to do this? But what do I know?

I have dinner outdoors in a lovely restaurant I stumble upon called Rouga, where I stuff my face with flattened chicken cooked with wild mushrooms, sage and cognac, followed by a free, perfect dessert of thick, creamy Greek yoghurt with crushed black cherries. As everywhere in Thessaloniki, the service is delightful, and more importantly sincere and I ponder whether we could solve the Greek crisis by placing all the call centres here. Kindness, sincerity and honesty are my enduring memories of this city. But then you just know they would give everybody a refund.

RAINING IN VENICE

If you are flexible about where you want to go in the world, then whichever month you book your bargain adventure, you can find somewhere amazing to thrill your travel tastebuds. But if your heart is set on a particular part of the world, then you need to consider the best time to go there for those important factors of cost and climate.

I did my European jaunt in October, which was great, but perhaps September would have been better, in terms of a combination of generally pleasant climes and decent non-peak prices. June has similar advantages, as does May if you're prepared to sacrifice a bit of sunshine for some big savings.

Travelling using the *Tripping* methods does work for those tied down by school holidays, however. Yes, your initial flight out of Britain will tend to be more expensive (though using my tips, you will still get the best deals) but if your next stepping stone is flying on from a country which takes its school/university holidays at a different time, you will no longer be paying over the odds. That's why a multi-centre jaunt can make economic sense if you are flying trans-continental to a country which has its low season during your own peak season. While there are definitely months where prices are generally lower, there are bargains available all year around which can be dug out using this function. Looking at flights to Miami, for instance, I found a school holiday-friendly £179 bargain from London in August, nestling next to a cheapest fare of £1,140 for the previous day. It's an eccentric market.

For the most expensive and cheapest months to fly to each destination, and how long in advance to take the plunge, I reckon you can rely on our trusty friends at Skyscanner. Check out 'best time to book' on their site. I hesitate to recommend an ideal month to visit a country. I've been to Tallinn in Estonia during the gorgeous and joyous white nights of high summer when it never gets really dark. But I've also been in the middle of the bleak midwinter, when you are lucky to grab four hours of light, and found January in the north Baltic just as magical. The daylight was brief but it was also pure, bright, clean and virginal, while the blizzard I trudged through, from one cosy basement to another in candlelit inns with open fires, was extraordinarily romantic. And it was extra-specially gorgeous to snuggle up in the warmth of a converted stables in a medieval merchant's house at the soporific Three Sisters Hotel. Equally I have holidayed in Puerto Rico on the edge of the rainy season. I loved the tropical storms and swimming in the pool or warm sea while fat globules of rain fell on my face from above. Never had I felt so happily immersed. Another rainy season, I got soaked to the skin riding a horse up a volcano in Costa Rica: visceral, elemental and beautiful. Summer may be a delight in Paris, London or Rome but cities can also be sappingly hot-and-sticky tourist hellholes. And then there are places like San Diego or Crete – lovely to visit all year round.

Despite all of this, here is a guide, with the proviso that these are the best times to go according to conventional wisdom, taking into account prices of flights, accommodation and weather. I'm not one for convention, so I'd definitely consider visiting these places outside the 'ideal' times, and often thems the dates when you can snaffle the tastiest deals. This is a subjective list, as expectation is the enemy of a carefree holiday. But it may help provide food for thought.

JANUARY/FEBRUARY

Egypt
Cape Town
The Philippines
Luang Prabang, Laos
Cambodia
Jamaica
Costa Rica
Buenos Aires
Prague
Zanzibar
China, the Yellow Mountains
Quebec City

MARCH/APRIL

Cyprus
Morocco
Amman
Nepal
Dubai
Panama
Lima
Rio de Janeiro
Singapore
Bologna
San Francisco
Dubrovnik

MAY/JUNE

Athens
Lisbon
Sofia
Budapest
Istanbul
Tel Aviv
Fez
Shanghai
Malaysia
Niagara
Malta and Gozo
Cuzco

JULY/AUGUST

Puerto Rico
Cartagena
Bavaria
Transylvania
Prague
The Azores
Northern Spain
Barcelona
Baku
Riga
Portland, Oregon
Warsaw

SEPTEMBER/OCTOBER

Aruba/Curacao/Bonaire
Mexico
New Orleans
Crete
Madeira
Madrid
Shanghai
Beirut
Corsica
Venice
Trieste
Marseille

NOVEMBER/DECEMBER

Guadeloupe
Colombia
Santiago
Antalya
Tunisia
Durban
Goa
Abu Dhabi
Vietnam
Burma
Amsterdam
Las Vegas

SUMMER & EASTER SCHOOL HOLIDAYS

It's easy to find bargains in the Easter and summer school holidays. I'll outline a route and how to find your own bargains in the walkthrough chapter, but here are a few examples if you are not keen on bobbing all over Europe for three or four weeks and want no more than three or four flights.

First things first, as you know, don't fly return and never fly in a straight line. This is especially true during the summer holidays. The cheapest return flight I could find to Europe was £138 to Brussels in peak season. But if you don't fancy a week in Belgium, how about this for a peak season deal? I found flights from London to sunny Bordeaux on 17th August for £31. After six glorious nights among the vineyards, grab a seat to Lisbon for a £20 two-night break to round off your holiday. Then it's £84 back home on 25th August. That's a grand total of £135 for a cultured and classy trip at the height of the summer season. Or how about this, eschewing the Mediterranean for a different kind of sun-kissed beach? I found flights from London to Cologne at the top of summer on 3rd August for £12. You can then spend a week enjoying the cultural delights of one of Europe's most cosmopolitan cities – and this fine city on the Rhine is surrounded by lakes and tons of beach clubs offering sandy delights for a snip. Sundown Beach Club at leafy Escher Lake is one of the best. This surreal experience will see you sunning yourself on 5,000 tons of sand, amid gently swaying palm trees, average daily highs of 75°F and lilting music to make you imagine you're in the Caribbean. Only the sight of Cologne's gorgeous Gothic cathedral across the lake will confirm otherwise.

After six nights, time to live it up like a Prussian aristocrat. I found flights to Riga, Latvia's sparkling and thrilling capital, at just £20 from Cologne. I would spend a couple of nights in this incredibly fun city before taking the 45-minute journey to the seaside spa town of Jurmala, a favourite in the past with everyone from Prussian duchesses to Soviet high fliers. Here it's as lovely and lively as anywhere on the Mediterranean, it costs a fraction, average temperatures are touching 70°F, but best of all you can expect bright sunshine until long after 10.30p.m, so you have a whole lot more time to top up your vitamin D levels. A flight back to London on the 17th was available for £32. That means this incredible two-week adventure sets you back just £64.

If you must have the steamy south then you can fly not to Riga but to Rome for the same price, £20 – but your flight back to London leaves a day earlier and costs £20 more at £52. That still means the whole caboodle will be just £84 return, which is a summer scoop by anybody's standards. Lastly, at the end of January there were still some amazing Easter deals out there. With Skyscanner I managed to dig out a flight from London to Legoland airport Billund in Denmark for £22 on 30th March, fly to Gdansk (which resembles a full-sized Legoland) for £9.20 on 3rd April, then six nights in lovely Pomerania before returning home on 9th April for £22. That's a 13-day Easter holiday Baltic jaunt for £51. And any extra expense you have in pricey Denmark will be more than compensated for in glorious Gdansk. here are some incredible bargains *whichever* time of year you fancy being footloose.

CHAPTER 6

ROME IS WHERE THE HURT IS...

So it's time I quit the Balkans for now. The Mediterranean has been bliss, especially anticipating the grey hell of November in England which I will be heading back to before too long. But the plan is to head back towards Europe's centre where there tend to be more and cheaper connections for the rest of my journey. That's the other thing, which I deal with on page 178: when you are booking a trip like this, you have to be careful not to end up heading up a cul-de-sac, a place where the only way out is back from whence you came. Punto Delgado, for example, in the Portuguese Azores looks amazing, but you are limited in your options unless you plan to head on to North America, which would certainly be an exciting way to make that trip.

So I need a hub airport next; it's either that or the Greek islands, which I could cheerily hop around on £15 flights until the end of the month, but that's not what this book is about (maybe next time!). The only hub city options around this time of year are onwards to Athens or Rome, both around the same price. I've never been to Rome, and it has some interesting connections, so off I head to the Eternal City.

Rome! Rome! Be excited Andrew! (Sorry, I promise never to refer to myself in the third person again. For now.) I mean it's Rome, by God, a city which should be on any traveller's bucket list, right? The capital of the world. Where everything we consider 'Western' began, pivot of the most incredible empire the world had ever seen. The epicentre of Christian culture, and the capital of Italy, home to the world's greatest historic, cultural and epicurean treasures. I mean, I know Liverpool fancies its chances, but if any place deserves the title God's Own City, surely this is it. So it's odd that out of all the cities I've visited, and all the cities I'm yet to see on this trip, this is the place for which I have the least enthusiasm. It's partly that I'm expecting Italian organised chaos and lack of tourist amenability on such a grand scale that it's tiring just imagining it. I've got images of Oxford Street during a tube strike, transposed on to a two millennial old backdrop. But mostly, I suspect, it's because I feel like I've been here before. Before I knew what England and Britain and abroad and foreign were, I knew about Rome. I'm a Roman Catholic, you see. And when you were a little Roman Catholic boy growing up in Gateshead in the 1970s, you knew about Rome before you even heard people slagging off London, our other capital. You heard so much about Rome and the Vatican and the Pope that frankly the whole place became unutterably boring. Your aunties went to Rome. Every bugger went to Rome. I felt like I spent my whole formative life being force-fed Rome, so consequently I had absolutely no interest in actually going to the place. Albania, Corsica, Estonia – now you're talking! But Rome? Nahhh. Who knows, maybe also there was unacknowledged resentment against a place which symbolised a religion which had made my childhood pretty unhappy on too many occasions and left guilty, self-loathing footprints on my psyche which I am still, many years later, fighting (with some success) to shake off.

Rome Ciampino Airport does nothing to blow away my preconceptions of organised chaos, grand Italian style. The airport itself is fine but outside in the car park it's a free for all – your guess is as good as mine as to which bus will get me to Ciampino train station and ferry me to the centre of Rome. I join a group of similarly bamboozled Brits and Aussies who have just flown in from London, and together we find a bus after about 45 minutes and then jump on to the first train to Popeville.

On the train, a crabby female ticket inspector asks us why we haven't had our tickets stamped, and also tells me I've bought a ticket for a service run by a different train operator. She conducts her conversation half with us and half looking towards the other (Italian) passengers on the train, rolling her eyes and shaking her head while catching the eyes of the other travellers. Tsk. She resembles a tut made flesh. Bloody tourists. We all refuse to get caught up in the drama of things and the other Brits and Aussies agree to get off the train at the next station, stamp their tickets, and get another train in half an hour.

'You are in a foreign country now,' she reprimands loudly so that the whole carriage will hear. 'You should respect our laws and customs.' That's told them. Bloody coming here, buying our tickets, spending your money, riding our trains. Nobody, much to her chagrin, argues back. Neither has anyone shown the slightest hint of anything other than confused politeness.

I decline her offer to vacate the train and instead tell her I will pay the penalty fare. She looks totally enraged by this.

'But... but...'

'Really, it's only five euros, it's nothing. Thank you though,' I say pleasantly. She stomps down the carriage sighing loudly and rolling her eyes in exasperation at the other passengers. Silly cow. Welcome to Rome. Fortunately things get better as I head to my hotel.

This particular trip taught me a lot about getting bargain luxury boltholes. It was never my intention to stay in cheap hotels for this trip. I like a bit of comfort, and the money I saved on flights I spent on other things. But of course it's up to you whether you do the same, or stay in hostels. Hotels have a similar predicament to airlines – how to fill unsold rooms/seats without lowering what is the perceived cost of a particular hotel/flight. Basically, empty rooms are money burned, so they sell them off for a fraction, but they prefer it not to be common knowledge. The best place to find these bargains I believe is on lastminute.com's Secret Hotels section, which I trialled in Rome.

They tend to be only good hotels using this service, because a two or three star or a ropey, overrated four or five star would have no problems slashing its prices if it had rooms to spare. So these are places with good reputations who want to sell off their rooms, kinda under the counter, if you like – so they don't tell you the name of the hotel you're getting, though they tell you how close your hotel is to a certain location so you know you won't be stuck out by the airport, unless you want to be. I want to be near Rome's central station, and I know this 'lovely, four star boutique hotel' is within 300 yards of the terminus. If you have the time or inclination, there are enough clues to work out which hotel you're getting (see the 'wherever I lay my hat' chapter) but I quite enjoy the element of surprise, spinning that hotel roulette wheel. So I take the plunge and book. As soon as your credit card is accepted, lastminute.com emails you details of your hotel.

Mine is the very lovely Royal Court Hotel, which more than lives up to its billing. This is a beautiful old Roman mansion house, lots of brass, cornflower yellow and dusky red, with nice Neoclassical touches. On top of this stately pile there's a gorgeous outside terrace, overlooking the rooftops of Rome. I look out over the city and that tingle of excitement you get in capital cities runs down my spine. The Royal Court cost me £120 for two nights, which is a snip by any standards. The cheapest I can find for this place online elsewhere is £180 on the hotel's own website, which beats the prices of hotels. com, trivago.com and the rest. I'm definitely won over to lastminute. com's Secret Hotels. I think you'll struggle to find luxury for less and it appeals to my sense of surprise and adventure as well as my love of a bargain.

I head out for lunch, and there is no mistaking that big city buzz which, for all the hassles and strains, I do miss when I'm out of London for too long. Rome is not multi-cultural, a world city, in the way that London, New York and Los Angeles are; it's still very, very Italian. But there is a confidence, a swing and a pace to this city. It's not so much a cockiness, just an absolute lack of self-doubt, which lets you that know that you are in one of the world's greatest cities. It reminds me of most capital cities. 'You can love me, you can hate me', they say, 'I really couldn't give a toss. Because I'm *me*.' That's kinda sexy.

After 14 days away I'm beginning to look a bit shabby, especially next to the immaculate Italian boys, and I notice a red-striped barber's pole on a side street next to my hotel, opposite the Prince Galles Hotel on Via Palestro. If you're in town and need a haircut, shave and beard trim, I couldn't recommend this place more highly, although at €30, these are not backstreet prices. Nor should they be: my barber turns out to be an artist, and I depart having gone from grim to glamorous. It's a beautiful old barber's shop, the sort they try to ape in Soho, Shoreditch or Manchester's Northern Quarter, but it's all far too gentrified these days to convince. This guy is the real deal, and as I peek inside for service, he waves at me from outside the restaurant next door where he's hoovering down a colossal plate of pasta and a major glass of red. Portly, in his sixties I'm guessing, with a contented, rosy cheeked face, pin stripe shirt, braces and brogues, plus slicked back, jet-black hair, he's a total dude. He gestures to me that he will be over in five minutes to cut my hair, and I ask the waitress at the restaurant to tell him to take his time, while I myself relax into a heaving plate of Italian meats. Some 45 minutes later I dive into his cushioned leather chair and sit back while this Italian master weaves his magic. My hair is made as sharp as a raven's beak, my beard evened to within a tenth of a millimetre. There is brass, leather and mirrors everywhere, and religious icon next to religious icon next to religious icon. It reminds me of the homes of my Auntie Hilda and my Auntie Mary CarPark and is oddly soothing and comforting. (Note: her surname wasn't really CarPark. I don't think car parks existed when surnames were invented. No, there were two Auntie Marys and this one of them lived next to a Car Park. Simple, see?) I'm not sure how I'd feel in a room full of Allahs or Shivas, but the effect of having lots of Virgin Marys, Jesuses, Popes and Saint Peters smiling benignly down on me is oddly soporific. I regress to a world where things were simple and certain. I remember gazing intently at these strange icons, statues and paintings when I was a little boy and feeling like they loved me. Sitting here having my hair rescued in Rome, I can see why. These aren't the 'fire and damnation' symbols I remember from later in my childhood. They really do seem to have painted love, forgiveness and – crikey – tolerance, into their eyes. But most of all, love. And as much as the religion that raised me now frequently appals me, I do remember that love; and the good things they taught us, about forgiveness, compassion, loving your fellow man as your brother or sister. It's just too bad so few of them practised what they preached. But then that observation is hardly ground-breaking these days. Still, in that moment, I really did feel a rosy glow of love. The eyes of those icons are almost subversive because when you stare into them, they say more than the Bible could ever say, more than the Catholic Church has ever had to say. They say more by saying less. All they really say is, well, love and be kind. And really, what more do we need to say? Do we need a structure or an ideology to remind us of this? Just focus on those eyes, then go out and live your life, and I believe things will fall gently into place.

At this point I was going to go into a diatribe about my visit back to the station and my attempt to find an ATM while being roundly insulted in bars and shops by the people I ask for help. But see, focusing on that word, 'love', even I can't bring myself to go into a rant about the epic rudeness of people in the Roman service industry. Put it this way, they make Parisians look like Teletubbies.

It's almost performance art, it's so breathtakingly, unnecessarily horrible. Oh, see. That didn't last long... I have a theory. Because I like Italians a lot. I have more Italian friends than you can shake a papal sceptre at (mainly because, as I'm sure you recall, I'm catnip to Italians). But let's face it, they're absolutely insane. I've worked out why. This is the home of pizza and pasta. The only way Italy functions as a state, rather than just hibernates in a drowsy carbohydrate haze, is because it mainlines bucketloads of coffee. Basically they are self-medicating to get through the day. Italians at play are generally frolicking gloriously in a carby, Aperol-spritzed fantasy world, but when the working week begins they ingest so many espressos that being in Italy is akin to being locked in a room full of cokeheads with bad childhoods and attachment issues. The slightest hiccup leads to scores of people getting involved, waving their hands, rolling their eyes, slapping their foreheads in exasperation. All because somebody dropped the hole-punch. Drama queen doesn't come close, as a description. They fucking love it. You know, it's funny and maybe even slightly adorable when you are watching it from a safe distance, but not when you are somehow embroiled in the bosom of the melee.

Romans are delightful so long as they are not required to do anything much which was invented post the Risorgimento in 1871. They basically can't cope with the modern world, whether it is driving, or working in a mall whilst chewing gum and trying to answer a polite question. Italy should have been left out of the last 150 years because when forced to participate, it behaves like a teenager forced to do homework when it would rather be hooked to the PlayStation. Which, y'know, is fair enough, when you absorb the beauty and timelessness of this place. If you really want to enjoy Italy, avoid anything modern which involves a degree of lucid and logical organisation. Go for the *passeggiata* and the *aperitivo*, the food, the architecture, the sex even. Stay away from malls and don't depend on cards, cashpoints or technology of any kind. The point of Italy, to non-Italians, is as a detox from the 21st century, and I'm a spoiled brat for not having realised this sooner.

There's a good and bargain Metro system in Rome, but by taking my SIM card out of my broken phone and sticking it into a cheap old mobile, then tethering them together... I can actually pretty much have one working mobile phone in two halves (why didn't I think of this earlier?!). So I can once again enjoy the delights of satnav, and I take a leisurely afternoon-long stroll from my hotel towards the Vatican City. Rome is grand and confusing by day, the strands of history interweaving, the classical and Neoclassical intertwined so that it's hard, for a plebeian like me, to be sure which is which.

When I finally cross onto the Papal turf, I must confess I'm feeling somewhat emotional. All my aunties, the real ones and the ones who were just some old bird from down the road, made pilgrimages here – I mean, that's what you do here, right? I just never thought for one second that I might be doing the same thing. They viewed Rome as the closest thing to heaven on earth, and I soon realise that this is not just any other city break for me either: if not a pilgrimage, then certainly a reckoning of sorts. I walk around her grand façades, designed to inspire fear as much as awe and I'm not really feeling the love. Just a cauldron of resentment boiling inside of me. I tell myself this is just a place, I mean you can't hate bricks and mortar or whatever the Papal palaces are built out of, can you? I've been to some beautiful religious places, where the sense of peace is profound. But I can't feel any love here. I really can't. Just bombast. I recall those people who have slated the reinvented Skopje for just that. That was the point of classical Roman architecture, and surely it's the point of Neoclassical. It's just a projection of power. I'm really struggling with the Vatican City, becoming overwhelmed by a tide of feelings, not all bad, about my Catholic childhood, which seem to have crystallized here. This is not what I anticipated nor wanted. I come across a poster protesting against plans to legalise gay marriage in Italy, and whereas once upon a time, I would have expressed delight that we are even having a discussion about such a thing, this time I find myself tearing at its corners. Ripping shreds off it. And hot tears are running down my face.

'You fucking bastards, you fucking cunts,' I hear myself saying. 'You're not gonna win this time.' Please forgive me for my self-indulgence. But in all its futility, it felt good. A catharsis I was not aware that I needed. And having shed my tears for a childhood lived in shame and fear and self-disgust, for the little lad who knew he was loved but was told by his 'teachers' and 'spiritual guides' that he would be cast out and no longer loved if people knew who he really was, for my friends who suffered too, and for the countless lives utterly destroyed by this nasty ideology, I felt better. The Vatican City is not beautiful to my eyes, whatever the aesthetics may say. But it didn't leave me with a sense of awe or fear, so it failed on its own terms. I wouldn't say I made my peace with it,

I just now find it largely irrelevant. I'd come back to Rome, but there's nothing left for me to see here.

I end my day at a pub called Garbo, a lovely twinkly, wink-winky, velvety gay bar, the closest there is to the Vatican City. As a den of immorality this place takes some beating; they're about to start their book club where 20 or so locals and expats will read chapters, passages or poems from their favourite books. They're a lovely lot, uniformly welcoming, gently flirtatious. It's not stuffy by any means and I'm chatting to an American lad with a ring through his nose, who came to the Eternal City to enter the priesthood but found another path. I chat with the ex-pats about the grand frustrations of life in the Italian capital. All agree, they can't live with it, can't live without it. I ask if many of the cardinals and bishops and priests from the Vatican City find their way in here.

'Oh no,' one tells me. 'We're far too chatty. That's not what they're looking for. They're much more likely just to head straight to the hard gay sex clubs.'

Rome! Go figure...

PITFALLS & HOW TO
TURN LEMONS INTO LEMONADE

The world of travel may be a bowl of cherries... but before you chomp right down, watch out for the stones. I made the mistakes – so you wouldn't have to.

AIRPORTS WHICH ARE NOWHERE NEAR WHERE THEY ARE MEANT TO BE

What's in a name? Sometimes your name can be misleading, as in Sue Barker, who is clearly not a dog. Other times, well, draw your own conclusions from Lloyd Grossman. As for my ex-colleague at National Vulcan, Debbie Goodhead; well, I really have no idea what she got up to in her spare time. Airport titles can be just as troublesome to the breezy traveller with an eye for a bargain. A bargain may not be such a bargain when you wind up 100 miles from your hotel at close to midnight, forced to pay £300 quid in taxis or sleep in a Serbian skip. Below is a list of the airports which are furthest from the city which bears their name, often thanks to the rebranding efforts of the low cost airline which flies there. London Oxford is not only nowhere near London but actually also a full seven miles from Oxford; Paris Beauvais is 54 miles from the French capital and Barcelona Girona is incredibly handy for Girona, but 58 miles from the city which most people fly there to get to.

It's a trap I fell into when I booked my flight out of Barcelona to Pisa, and actually discovered I was flying out of Girona. As you know, I turned those lemons into lemonade and thrust myself into lovely Girona.

So if you're hopping around Europe and you land at Beauvais for two or three nights, you can either spend a bomb and end up in a stream of horrible tourist traps as you attempt to get to grips with the French capital, or give it the old Gallic shrug and delight in the fact that Beauvais is in the heart of the gorgeous Picardy region, with its beautiful medieval villages and endless, rolling skies. *Oui, oui* and thrice *oui*. As for London Oxford, well I will defy anyone who doesn't agree that London is the world's most fantabulous international city, but if you're flying in for a few nights, why not visit England and Oxford. London is not England and England is not London, and never confuse the two; and hooray for that on every count. I chose to make my home in London, not England. But that doesn't mean I don't like to visit my former home country. Oxford and the Cotswolds is a fine experience for two or three nights. Why do these low cost airlines feel the need to gild the lily? Watch out for these misleading titles, but don't discount these bargain airports. They may actually conceal a real travel gem.

THE 10 AIRPORTS FURTHEST AWAY FROM THEIR 'HOME CITY'

1. Paris Vatry – over 100 miles from cental Paris, an estimated two hours nine minutes. Serves Châlons-en-Champagne in northeastern France (*see* page 49)
2. Oslo Torp – 73 miles, around one hour and 28 minutes to Norway's capital
3. Munich West (Memmingen) – 70 miles, one hour 17 minutes from the city centre

4. Frankfurt (Hahn) – 68 miles, over an hour's drive
5. London Oxford – 61 miles, an hour and a half to central London
6. Stockholm (Skavsta) – 60 miles from central Stockholm
7. Barcelona (Girona) – 58 miles from central Barcelona
8. Barcelona (Reus) – 58 miles from central Barcelona
9. Paris (Beauvais) – 54 miles from central Paris
10. Dusseldorf (Weeze) – 49 miles from central Dusseldorf

THE 10 AIRPORTS CLOSEST TO THEIR 'HOME CITY'

Forget public transport, hop in a cab and fly into town.

1. Taipei Sungshan – 3 miles from central Taipei
2. Salt Lake City – 3 miles from central Salt Lake City
3. San Diego – 3 miles from central San Diego
4. Tallinn – 3 miles from central Tallinn
5. Belfast (George Best) – 3 miles from central Belfast
6. Wellington – 4 miles from central Wellington
7. Honolulu – 4 miles from central Honolulu
8. Lisbon – 4 miles from central Lisbon
9. Bucharest Otopeni – 4 miles from central Bucharest
10. Mexico City Juarez International – 4 miles from central Mexico City

BAD FLIGHTS

As with badly located airports, bad flights are often the ones we leap at, blinded by excitement at the thought of a flight which costs less than your left sock (unless you are posh and wear mohair or something). Then we realise it leaves at 6.05 a.m. or lands when the whole city has shut until dawn. Just be aware of these but don't automatically write them off.

I left both Girona and Pisa barely after dawn, but the Hotel Bologna in Pisa offered a free airport shuttle, while Girona Airport is so close to the city centre, and taxis so cheap, it was not really a hardship to get to the flight on time. Nicer still was arriving somewhere before lunch with a full day to explore the city, or even have a post-prandial siesta. My latest arrival was in Warsaw, and the city was still pumping and primping itself for me, plus I sped to my hotel in a super cheap cab. These things matter less in cheaper countries where you can jump in a taxi, rather than in Norway where you know the only option other than bankruptcy is to get the local bus or train, assuming it's running.

INSURANCE

I know, just that word and already your gaze is drifting from the page. Imagine how I felt, insuring lifts and cranes for a living. Or not, as it turned out. This, however, is where it makes sense to invest a little. When you've experienced this way of travelling once, you're bound to want to do it again, so spend a little more on an annual multi-trip policy.

And get a decent insurance policy for a few quid more. Life is too short to be spent reading the small print of insurance policies. Have a gander and see which policies *Which* is recommending, and pick one that doesn't include huge excesses, especially if you're taking expensive electrical equipment with you. I think through the whole of my trip I maybe experienced in total a one-hour flight delay, which is incredible if you have ever used the British public transport 'network', but look for policies that pay out for flight delays and missed connections, just in case. Keep in mind that if you buy two connecting flights in one bundle on Kiwi.com, they will pay out if one of your fights is cancelled and leads you to miss the follow-on flight. We definitely heart Kiwi.com. And let's keep this between ourselves, but please Google their owner. He's really hot. So they are better than Virgin in that way too.

COST OF LIVING

What's the point of getting a bargain flight if once you get there it's £85 for a bag of chips, not even with a pickled onion on the side? If you're on a budget, keep an eye on the living costs of the cities you're visiting. You could book an all-bargain trip around Poland, Spain and Bulgaria if you like. Or if you're desperate for Scandinavia, balance it out with some cheaper destinations across the Baltic Sea or in the Balkans. Website Numbeo, the biggest internet cost-of-living database, is a treasure when figuring out the comparative cost of living between two towns, countries or entire continents to find the best places to live like Croesus on a McDonald's budget.

There are many ways to measure how expensive a city is to visit, so it's a little subjective.

If it's a bargain you're after in Europe, best you head east to cities which still feel undiscovered while offering five-star experiences at three, two or even one star prices. Here are my top ten bargain world cities (well, including one region), chosen not just for price but also for the quality of the experience.

Goa	Phnom Penh	Auckland
Kiev	Budapest	Quito
Bucharest	Asuncion	
Sofia	Mexico City	

MOBILE PHONES & CASH CARDS

Nothing, perhaps not even my passport, was more important to me on my trip around Europe than my mobile phone(s) and cash cards. When my mobile phone decided it was having a bit if a midlife identity crisis, and it wasn't a phone after all, I discovered a few days later that I had, ingeniously, packed a shabby old phone as a back-up. Well done me! I was able to stick my SIM card in my old phone and tether out to my newer device through Wi-Fi, allowing me to do most of the things I had been able to do earlier, albeit in a long-winded fashion. Satnav and maps were available to me, saving me a fortune in taxis whenever I got lost two minutes from my hotel, as is my wont, and I was constantly able to have contact with my friends, which came in handy when I had too many painkillers and needed to know which city I was in.

You can be as rich as Princess Michael of Kent but still be skint if you don't have access to readies. My biggest fear when I was away alone, was being mugged or losing my cards and mobile phone. How would I ever manage without access to cash and no one to pick up the slack for me? No one to call for help? In the end, I set up a new account with cash card access, to run alongside my two free current accounts. And there was my essential Barclaycard. I would definitely recommend having a decent credit card if you're staying in various hotels over a few days in America, not least because they will each fleece you for a big deposit, which they may or may not repay within a few days of checking out, depending on their mood at the time. I have had plenty plunder my accounts in the past without even telling me they were going to do this. As well as being rude, this is also massively inconvenient. Don't ever, EVER, hand over a debit card to these leeches if you've budgeted carefully for each step of your trip. (And don't expect better treatment from big chains, they're worse, and take out greedier amounts. I'm talking to you, W Hotels.)

In the end, having four cards may have seemed like overkill, but by the end of the month I had snapped one card and left the other behind in a machine in Skopje. When I was down to two cards I took only one out with me on any given night in case of mishaps. All of this reminds me of my next pitfall, or more a way to avoid it...

SAFETY, POCKETS & PUTTING THINGS IN THEIR PLACE

I hold my hands up. I'm generally an extremely disorganised man trying desperately to be organised. I also tend to panic a great deal and imagine I've lost stuff. In general, things don't often leap out of your pockets, like horny salmon during mating season, of their own accord. Here's a tip: always keep your most important, treasured things in specific pockets of your coat or bag, a place specially allocated for them. Like the Royal Family, they should all travel separately. So please keep some of your cards in your bag, some in your coat, some in your trousers. Then, whatever happens, you will have something upon your person. Normally I spend hours at airport security freaking out that I have lost my passport/mobile/credit card. This time, my passport only ever lived in one place, one pocket of my bag.

KEEPING WELL

Nothing screws up your journey like getting ill. Prevention is the most important thing, and if you're getting a lot of flights you're going to be around lots of other people's germs within a confined space. I managed to fight off an early cold by hammering Berocca and other soluble vitamin cocktails, which I would down before getting on flights to keep my immune system sturdy. Definitely pack some.

My numero uno essential travel item, my absolute hero travel product, is a bottle of Cold and Flu Defence spray. On my first flight I was being sneezed all over by a man in the row behind, but managed to avoid getting really sick by spraying myself.

Always pack some cheap antihistamines in case you find yourself allergic to Moldovan washing powder; and sure, painkillers can be bought anywhere, but carry an emergency pot in case you are struck down when the shops are shut. Lastly, look after your mental well-being, especially if you're traveling alone. Be kind to yourself. Whatsapp is an invention up there with Marmite and karaoke in my book, a thing of pure joy which is as delightful and free as wild blackberries. For me, to be able to chat with your loved ones any time you're near some Wi-Fi is truly the gift that just keeps giving.

CHAPTER 7
BRIEF ENCOUNTER

I know it will be painful going from the still sun-dappled European south to October in the north. But I am not ready for *this*. Brussels Charleroi Airport is cloaked in freezing fog. I depart the plane from Rome coatless, as I have been pretty much throughout my journey so far, apart from a couple of nippy nights in Skopje and Barcelona. Stepping into the gloom of the airport environs, I feel my blood turn to ice popsicles.

Arrival at Brussels Midi Station, lunchtime on a Tuesday is hardly any more inviting. Empty and unheated, with indecipherable ticket machines, nobody here, nothing appearing to work and nowhere to go for help, the Belgian capital is not exactly filling me with glee. I can't say, at this point, that I'm disappointed to be spending only one night here. I stand in driving rain on a freezing platform for almost an hour waiting for a train that seems like it will never come, until I finally climb on board a depressing carriage, and we chunter past a landscape that makes North Manchester, Outer Bradford, Croydon, Swindon and Stoke look positively

Californian in their cheeriness. Even The Smiths would have balked at this. From behind a vista of Belgian post-industrial decay poke the glittering turrets of the Grand Place, one of Europe's most baubled, embellished and sparkling squares evoking a glorious Belgian past which never actually happened. I'm not sure if there is such a decayed place within eyeshot of Westminster or Big Ben. We pass the most forlorn-looking Ferris wheel in the world. It's so despondent, this could surely be some kind of Belgian joke, as dark as their smoky sweet Chimay Blue. When I arrive in the Brussels suburb of Schaerbeek, the sky is even blacker than the beer, and I run through an unrelenting rainstorm so powerful it could flatten Tintin's quiff and drop off my bags at my hostel (yes that's right, a hostel!) and then, because the manager has warned me most places shut their doors at 3 p.m., leg it back through the watery tumult to the nearest bar and restaurant.

This, it turns out, is the bar and restaurant of Belgium's beautiful, shiny, new National Train Museum, opened just three weeks since. I crash in from the storm like the Flying Scotsman, into an Art Nouveau world of starched tablecloths, polished steel and brass, red leather seats, high ceilings and golden glowing lamps. I warm my soul with mussels steeped in dark beer, shallots and cream, with plenty of crusty bread and salty butter to mop up the juices. I follow this with waffles, ice cream and hot chocolate sauce.

OK, it's time to address the 'boring Belgium' thing. Never in the history of spurious international observations – and I've chanced my arm with more than a couple – has a country been so unfairly maligned as has Belgium for being allegedly boring. Thankfully, because the Belgians are a bit twisted and dark and really rather masochistic, they do tend to revel in this entirely inappropriate label. Belgium is fucking weird, quite frankly. Not crazy, like Italy. *Weird*. Brussels has more than a passing similarity to the similarly strange Skopje. In fact, in many ways, Macedonia is the Belgium of the Balkans, overlooked, underestimated and unloved. Belgium, like Macedonia, was once a geographical/ethnic no man's land, coveted by all its neighbours. Like Belgium it owes its existence to a historical compromise, which it was hoped (in vain, in Belgium's case) would prevent its neighbours from fighting for control of its strategically vital lands. Britain backed the creation of Belgium in 1830 because it didn't want such a nearby land falling into the hands of the frightful French; meanwhile, the locals had had enough of being patronised by their previous rulers, the Dutch. Since then this cobbled-together nation has incredibly survived two World War invasions, and somehow held together in a warring federation of Flemish Flanders, Francophone Wallonia and polyglot Brussels. Nobody seems really sure why Belgium has continued to exist, because nobody much likes it, particularly its citizens. Flemish and Wallonian Belgians each toy with the idea of separation; they are not much like one another, after all. Their loyalties tend to lie with their own regions, rather than some notional Belgium but it pootles along, doing crazy Belgian things like, at one point acquiring a massive empire and now accidentally becoming the de facto capital of Europe. Now that's one *dark* joke. And for that reason, and just the overarching sense of the obscure in this strange little corner of Europe, I do find myself rather loving it. This is definitely a country which belongs in the bargain bin. It's what a Californian might describe as a 'hot mess' but I'm not sure if any Californians have ever been here.

And so, now that I've largely survived the rain, I feel it is a shame that I'm here for only one night. The Belgians knew that when it came to climate, or scenery, or historical glory, they were fighting a losing battle with more, erm, glamorous parts of the world. So they set about becoming good at other stuff, like making chocolate and beer and the world's loveliest comfort food. Compensation, if you like, for the rest. But blimey they got good at that. And consequently Belgium, and more specifically Brussels, became world capital of cosiness.

I tell my hotel manager, 'You do "cosy" very well here.'

He throws a wry glance at the violent grey storm whipping across the empty streets of Schaerbeek outside, and shrugs.

'Well, we have to!'

The Belgians are weird people, and I like and relate to them for that. In one bar I visit later, I meet Michael from Portugal, who despite the climate has moved here from Lisbon and is conducting his own private love affair with Brussels. I ask him what the Belgians are like. 'The Walloons are like French people, but nice, and the Flemish are like Dutch people, but soft,' he tells me. 'It's like all of the good bits about France and Holland with none of the attitude.' I think Michael may have just pointed out a spectacular improvement, right in the heart of Europe. The people of Brussels are connoisseurs, who appreciate the finer things in life, but don't take themselves too seriously.

History has contrived to place Belgium in some unexpected situations. It even managed to nab itself a humongous colonial empire in the heart of Africa, the Belgian Congo, 76 times bigger than the country itself. The Flemish and Walloons, once persecuted nations themselves, got up to a lot more than just drinking Um Bongo in the Congo. That's when the country showed itself to be somewhat less convivial than the Belgium we know today, with possibly the cruellest colonial regime of any European power. Maybe countries are like people. You have to be wary of the ones who don't know who they are, because they can be capable of practically anything. So no, Belgium is not boring. It's possibly the most fucked up and fascinating place in Europe, with apologies to Macedonia and, naturally, my home country, England. As I write this, Brussels is in 'lockdown' following intelligence about a threat from Islamist terror groups. During raids across the city on a Sunday evening, authorities asked the local populace to refrain from mentioning any nearby raids on social media. Thousands responded by tweeting pictures of cats – Surrealism on a scale as big as the Grand Place or Captain Haddock's beard. Rik Coolsaet, terrorism expert at Ghent University, commented: 'Brussels is the city of René Magritte. So this kind of Surrealism is part of our reaction. I don't think you'd see the same in France or the US.' The Belgian police then got in on the act, tweeting the words 'thank you' alongside a picture of a police bowl filled with cat biscuits.

After lunch, with a belly full of love, I brave the walk back to my hostel, and find that the storm had subsided. I'm staying at the Train Hostel, as bizarre, cosy and delightful a place to lay your head as any in Europe, I'm fairly sure. Just a few weeks old, it's eccentric, or perhaps lunatic is a better word. Owner Nicolas Kervyn spent, I suspect, a small fortune dropping gorgeous old wood and steel train carriages on to the roof of a four storey, 19th-century Belgian townhouse. There is also an entire sleeper carriage, from the golden age of railways, which you can hire out and sleep in with your mates, or share with strangers. The entire, beautiful, quirky edifice is done out with seats, tables, clocks, sinks, blinds and livery from rail's glorious past. It almost makes you long to be on an actual real-life moving train. Until you remember you are British and the sheer screaming hell of your last attempted journey. If you are British and you want to go somewhere that's not where you actually are right now, and you live within one hour of an airport, it only makes sense to fly somewhere (preferably abroad, which will always have better transport) rather than endure the unedifying, emotionally exhausting, humiliating task of braving our trains, buses or motorways. That's why most Brits know more about Spain or Greece than they do about a town an hour down the road.

There are over 200 beds here in the Train Hostel, and you can spend practically nothing if you like for a night in a shared bunk bed carriage, or you can do like me, and book yourself into the rooftop suite, an entire carriage to yourself, with big soft double bed, stand up power shower and real recycled fixtures and fittings from beautiful old steamers. It's truly gorgeous, breezily romantic – like the bracing last scene between Celia Johnson and Trevor Howard in *Brief Encounter*, when they know their time is up. There are also suspenseful Hitchcockian elements, redolent of *Strangers on a Train*, which add to the sense of drama and romance. This would be a delightfully quirky place to spend a honeymoon. And you know, if all you want to do is eat *moules*, followed by chocolate, and then make love to your newly installed other half, I can't think of a finer place to come. Although you would always pretty much find me on a beach somewhere, as a cold weather alternative it's a dreamy evocation of romantic bliss.

The carriage suite is placed so that its *derrière* is hanging over the edge of the building. The overall effect is that of a train which has come hurtling off some Belgian viaduct and crashed on to the roof. With one third of your bedroom hanging perilously off the fourth storey of a converted Belgian mansion, it's a pretty impressive sight. Quirky doesn't quite suffice when describing Brussels.

My suspended bed is too cosy and inviting to be left alone, so with a bellyful of bodacious Belgian grub inside me, I clamber in. As I drift off, I once again hear the rain rattling on the carriage roof and I'm happy. But it's bittersweet. It would be lovely to share this with a special someone. Come to think of it, an anyone. To be big spoon or little spoon. Sigh!

Rested after forty winks, I spend my one and only Belgian night around the icy Grand Place. This place was flattened to a steaming pile of rubble by the French in 1695, as it was caught in yet another of the interminable wars between a grumpy, pre-revolutionary France and its pesky northern neighbours. Only the Town Hall façade survived but the locals did a pretty good job of dollying this place up and making it sparkle like an Antwerp diamond. It actually manages to out-frou-frou most of France's major cities, with an unexpectedly harmonious blend of Gothic, Baroque and Louis XIV architecture. It is as bombastic, showy-offy and nonsensical as Skopje's mismatched architectural hotchpotch. But they didn't have social media back then, so everybody just got on with it.

The Belgians have made a career out of flying under the radar, and quietly doing Frenchy kinds of things, but arguably slightly better. Perhaps freed from the history and expectation of the French cookery straightjacket, they've managed to accrue more Michelin stars per head of the population than France. Not that that means much, in my opinion. So dinner, just off the Grand Place, is at the Taverne du Passage. It has that red and yellow glow that Brussels' restaurants seem to favour, and the smells of steak and prawns and beer really do warm the cockles of my heart after the icy freeze of the Grand Place. You need a lot of comforting in Belgium and so consequently pretty much all Belgian food falls into that category. Dinner is a fat tomato for starters, cut all jaggedy in proper British Seventies style, innards scooped out and filled with North Sea shrimps, parsley and mayonnaise and served with bread and more salty butter. Back home, they'd call this 'retro'. But the Belgians are a million miles above such food faddism. They still dish out their vol-au-vents and there ain't nothing kitsch or knowing about it. Good food is good food, whatever the decade. I have no idea why Belgium's national dish *waterzooi* has never transcended its boundaries because this is a dish to gladden the soul of the weariest gourmet. It has been described as a 'confusion' of a soup and a stew, packed with vibrant bright vegetables, leeks and carrots, tarragon, butter, vermouth, stock, cream, egg yolks, pepper and parsley. Though it originally was made using white fish, here it features tender chicken breast. This is simple food, and the quality of the ingredients sings. Profiteroles complete my feast, black-dark chocolate and thick vanilla ice cream. After this, I will forgive Belgium its climate.

It's a short hop to my last stop of the night, a famous Belgian gay bar where they have haystacks and a rangy, hairy, bare-chested barman, plus some rooms out the back you might rather not know about. It's a world away from the supercilious, superior and sleazy scene of some of Europe's other capitals. Well, yeah, there is a bit of sleaze but it feels quite oddly wholesome.

It's the nearest a gay cruise bar can come to a traditional English 'local', feeling like everyone here has a connection with everybody else, and let's face it they probably have. But there's a sense of humour about the place, a sense of camaraderie.

I'm not here on the pull. Yeah, right! No, really! But I am welcomed into this friendship group and lavished with warmth and non-sexualised attentiveness. Well maybe it's a little sexualised, but I'm being modest, and I'm knocking on a bit, so forgive me for being a little relieved. Anyone who is over 40 will know what I mean by this; whenever anyone makes a blatant pass at you, whether they are a neighbour, the woman selling stamps in the Post Office, your bank manager or a Big Issue seller, your initial emotional reaction, before horror and fury and 'How dare you, that's so inappropriate' kicks in, is 'Hey, still got it! Never lost it!' So it's nice, and I'm enjoying the attention, but not really fancying anyone apart from this one bloke, who comes in with a broad, cheeky, affable smile, and then proceeds to get inebriated, and ever cheekier. He's definitely got the loveliest face in the room. You can see he loves a bit of a hoo-hah, in a humorous way, but you can also see from his open, honest face that he's a good lad. A nice fella. He's out of my league, I decide, and crack on with my night, only occasionally chuckling over his antics. As the bell goes for closing time, he comes towards me, a little unsteady on his feet, with the happy smile gone.

'Why didn't you speak to me?' he demands. 'I was looking at you all night and you spoke to everyone but me.'

'Really? Well, I can never speak to people I find very attractive. And I had no idea. I'm sorry,' I tell him. He stomps off towards the exit. While I've been indoors a wintery blanket has fallen over Brussels and, stepping out of the bar on to snow upon ice, he slips and I grab hold of him as he's about to go arse over tit. He still manages to look furious at me but he's clinging on to a lamppost like a Liverpool fan clings on to the past.

'Are you genuinely pissed off with me?' I ask, kind of half incredulous and half chuffed.

'Yes,' he pouts, believably but kinda adorably.

'Look, you are pissed mate. Are you e OK getting home?'

'Yes!' he thunders. He sets off, slips, and this time actually goes arse over tit. I help him to his feet and he softens a little.

'Look I have to get a taxi to my hotel, you're too tipsy to walk. Let me drop you off.'

It's only five minutes to his place in the cab but long enough for a nice little kiss. He invites me in, but I decline. Yes, really. It's not that I'm not a slag, just that I have to be up early for my flight the next day. I head back to my solitary rooftop train carriage a little sad I don't have my cheeky Flemish friend with me, but invigorated and glowing from the experience, as Brussels twinkles prettily in the dark. I've been around long enough to know that there is value in quitting while you are ahead. Something I seldom do. When I get in, I tuck myself into my cosy rail carriage bed and the phone rings. It's him. We chat for a couple more hours. It's lovely. One night in

Brussels but not quite a one night stand. Freezing Belgium has been like a warm hug after all. Before sleep I say 'Thank you universe!' and hunker down to dream of my handsome Belgian Brief Encounter.

PACKING IT

So you've booked your flights and you're ready to go, are you reader? Well I've got two words for you; fanny pack.

I know, hilarious, right? I shall never tire of hearing middle-aged Americans in velour travel tracksuits at airports saying things like, 'Honey, where did you put my antacid tablets?' 'Oh Leonard, how many times do I have to tell you – they're in my fanny pack.' When Americans say 'fanny packs', they mean 'bum bags'. But then you daren't say 'bum bag' in the USA, lest they think you are talking about the bag of a homeless person.

Anyway, back in the day, when life was simple and airlines didn't trick you into paying massive fees for your luggage, the bum bag/fanny pack was little more than an outdated fashion curio worn only by short-haired Dutch ladies with big earrings and tight jeans, and Italian would-be lotharios with swishy, swooshy, swept-back hair, denim pedal pushers and dodgy deck shoes.

I did own a bum bag briefly, but spent my time constantly worried that someone would half-inch my travellers' cheques out of it because it was worn, impractically, round the back. Eventually I took to wearing mine around the front, which I guess technically made it a ball bag instead, which though infinitely more sensible, was perhaps awkward to market given the name. Had I been a woman then it would indeed have been a fanny pack though, or perhaps a vag-bag which I think has a definite ring to it. It might be the time to revisit this idea. Hey, *Dragons Den*!

Anyway, I stopped wearing my bum bag after an unfortunate incident on a train when I was 23, while I was wearing my bum bag non-conformistly around the front under a long blue T-shirt which covered it just around my groin area. Hungover, close to being sick and passing through on the way to the cheap seats, I was thrown forward and hurtled towards Swindon as the train jolted to a halt, and my groin/bum bag, covered by said T-shirt, was thrust inadvertently into the face of a posh Home Counties lady bending over her table to do *The Times* crossword. The look of pure revulsion as she confronted my sweaty bloodshot face and massive groinal protrusion was enough to put me off bum bags for life. Which is a shame because I love practical fashion. Every time I visit Blackpool I invest in an umbrella hat. I have six in my wardrobe, all colours and designs, just waiting for the day they come into fashion and conquer the world, as they surely one day must.

So what is the point of this meandering schlep around another of my many lifetime humiliations? Well, the ridiculous world of airline baggage fees has made practical fashion more useful than ever. Wearable luggage is the antidote. Pack a medium-sized cabin bag, and let your wearable luggage do the rest. There are even ones which you can carry as a bag right up until you go through the gate, and then you unzip it, and sling it on as a coat. Some say it's a big raised middle finger to luggage fees. Personally I have no problem with these fees so long as I'm not paying them. In fact I like them. Every dumb ass stupid *TOWIE/Geordie Shore/Made in Chelsea* cast member or wannabe who gets clobbered for these fees makes my flight cheaper. Long live the stupid, I say, and those with more money than sense. Popular brands of wearable luggage are Stuffa, Jaktogo and Bagket;

search on Amazon and eBay for the best deals. Packing for this trip taught me a lot. To avoid baggage fees, I had to pretty much make sure I had everything I needed within the confines of a standard cabin bag, which is not very big and officially, if they are nasty and weigh you (which nobody did), usually no more than 10kg in weight. That required me to be efficient. Me and efficient are not typical bedfellows. Anyway, here's what I learned. True, 10kg is not a lot for a month's travel, but I got by surprisingly easily. It required me to know where everything was, which was a nice feeling for one so disorganised. It also meant I sailed in and out of little airports, I barely encountered a single problem at airline security and early morning flights were not the nightmare they have been in the past: with a five-minute security check in a small airport with few queues, I could risk arriving an hour before take-off, though I prefer more time to avoid panics. Of the low-cost airlines, Ryanair is miles ahead of its rivals when it comes to baggage allowance, offering a very generous two bags, a standard cabin-sized wheelie-on (the type I used) 55x40×20cm as well as an additional decent sized travel bag, 35×40×20cm. I first travelled with Ryanair about ten years ago, and it was not a particularly pleasant experience. While the Irish carrier boomed, it strangely seemed to have a business model which incorporated general shittiness almost as part of its brand strategy. It certainly got them attention. This has all changed. Apart from marvellously flying me between exquisite European cities for less than the price of a bad burger meal, I found the service extremely pleasant, at times even enjoyable. Cabin crew were lovely and on non-full flights (most of them) it was easy, after take-off, to move to a row of empty seats and stretch out. Even if you can't, seat pitch is a very pleasant 30–34cm, which means more legroom than on British Airways full price flights in some cases. Of the other carriers, Vueling and Jet2 offer pretty much identical main cabin bag sizes as Ryanair but no second bag; EasyJet main cabin bag is annoyingly slightly smaller, making it more difficult to hop between airlines, and there is no second free bag. Wizz Air is even more complicated, allowing you one main cabin bag of 42×32×25cm. You can upgrade to a large cabin bag for between €7.5 and €20, but in most cases that's more expensive than the flights I was taking. Oddly, however, if you take priority boarding, which costs a mere €3–€4, you are then allowed a second bag pretty much identical in size to the first (40×30×18cm). Confusing, huh? Anyways, I shelled out for the priority boarding on my Wizz Air flights, and took through the two same bags I had with me on my Ryanair flights, which technically put me over their baggage limits, but I encountered no problems and no charges, with my priority boarding sticker seeming to act like a magic charm.

Incidentally, in general airport staff, be they security or airline, tended to be a lot more easy-going and less tied to the letter of each rulebook once I left Britain. But where possible it's best to stick to the rules to avoid unnecessary disruption or expense.

So to packing; my usual practice of tipping everything I own into a suitcase, and then using only half of the gear, would clearly not wash. Your most important travel items are:

Passport
Travel tickets
Credit cards
Mobile phone and chargers
Keys

Everything else is gettable elsewhere. Take your insurance documents on your iPad or mobile phone. I love books and travel guides but download them Kindle style, or research your cities online as and when you land using your hotel's free Wi-Fi. I couldn't have crammed ten city guides into my bag, even if I *had* known where I was off to. If you are going to take one indispensable guide, then obviously this is the only one worth bothering with. Clever Ryanair, who are becoming real travel heroes, allow you to download tickets and boarding passes to your mobile phones these days so there is even less to carry with you. If you're scatterbrained like me, lists are the key to non-stressful packing. I've been using the same list for nearly ten years now, and it means I arrive at my destination with all the essentials. Once in my early twenties I left for a night flight to Cyprus, drunk as a Lord, and forgot to put all of my carefully ironed clothes into my case. I didn't even notice that it felt light. So you are learning from the world's least practical man here. It was nice, however, to come home to a pile of ironed clothes, though I did whiff a bit by then.

Health when you're away is dealt with on page 123, but most things can be grabbed wherever you are (often more cheaply than at home). It's worth packing stuff you might need in the middle of the night, however. Souvenirs and gifts are out I'm afraid, dear, which will at least make your trip cheaper. Don't forget your multi-plug for use all over the world, a portable charger is really handy and always bring your earphones of course. Music really can soothe the savage, travel-weary heart.

CHAPTER 8

THE GHOSTS OF GDANSK

On my first and last morning at the Train Hostel, I wake up, sneeze, and stot my head off the sharp corner of some wooden furniture. 'Ouch that hurts,' I confirm before adding, 'Ouch, that *really* hurts.' It doesn't really matter what I do from that point on. It's going to be one of *those* days. I should have stayed in bed, except that I can't, because I'm about to catch a flight for my first-ever trip to Poland.

Sure enough, everything that can go wrong does go wrong. Every marginal decision I make, every time I choose B over A or vice versa, I should have picked the other option. I've timed it to perfection, so that I have three and a half hours before I need to board my flight from Brussels Charleroi Airport. But as I drag my bags down to the ground floor and confess I can't find my room card which I used to get in my room the night before, the receptionist looks very upset like she may cry.

'I just thought it was a piece of plastic. Is it important?' I ask.

'Yes, I think so,' she says, nodding gravely.

Oh crikey, I've lost the Koh-i-noor diamond of plastic, microchipped key cards. While I search high and low for it in my suite, I miss my train to Brussels Midi, get the first train in that direction, get off en route because it isn't going to Midi – it's going to Zuid, which then turns out to have been Midi after all, just in Flemish instead of Wallonian or French or whatever – then I miss the connecting train.

One missed connection begets another missed connection, begets another, begets rising panic. One more slip up and I will miss the flight to Gdansk. And not just to there, but also to all the destinations I booked onwards from there. Today is shaping up to be a disaster. I opt to flag a cab rather than run around looking for the taxi shuttle at Brussels Midi station, which appears to have a different visage to the one it had when I arrived yesterday. Perhaps yesterday I arrived at the Flemish version and today I'm departing from the Wallonian spot. I grab a cab but he has to wait for his customer to return with payment for the last journey. Several taxis fly by while I wait for the missing fare payer. Finally a sweating, flustered British bloke emerges, brandishing cash. Huh. Typical! I get in and impress the driver with the urgency this trip has. Do I want it metered or set at 100 euros, he asks. Whaaaaaaat? That sounds like a lot for a 43-mile journey. I've read in my guidebook always to insist on metered cabs. As the fare soars over 100 euros, and then 150 euros, I actually have no idea how long it will take to get to the airport but my clever map app reckons about one hour. With traffic moving at the pace of the plot of *Mad Men*, I'm not so sure. In its bloody dreams. The driver delights in telling me I should have taken his offer of 100 flat with no clock. 'Well why didn't you tell me then, you fucker,' I mumble to myself. Then the phone rings; it's the sweaty Englishman, and he reckons he has left his Eurostar ticket and passport in the cab. We find the ticket. 'Shall we take it back to him?' asks the driver, clearly revelling in his place at the centre of two worlds of pain.

'No we bloody won't,' I tell him. This is my cab now. I can hear the man effing and jeffing at the driver. I take the phone off him. 'Look mate, get them to print you a new one.' He continues to swear.

'Such a shame,' says my smug driver. 'Such a nice guy and a great tipper.' I grimace. Are we there yet or not?

At Charleroi, I hand over 160 big ones. 'You should have gone on the meter as I suggested, mate,' says the driver.

'Fuck off before I batter you to death with my adapter plug and strangle you with its cord,' I tell him. Actually, that's a lie. Instead I thank him through gritted teeth. I do believe that negativity attracts negativity, and I'm becoming like Victor Meldrew. If there is a path to walk down en route to check in, I find the one with five American hipster student girls straddled across the passage, arms all linked, and with the urgency one attaches to filling out an end-of-year tax form. Grrrrrr! At security, there are three equal queues but I've got a feeling for queue number three. I jump in, just as an extra lane opens for queues one and two, and half of queue three's staff head off for a cheeky cig. Agggghhhhhh! I get to the gate, expecting to see the last passengers' tail feathers disappear into the plane.

'Oooh, you've got ages,' says the lovely gate girl. 'We are well behind today. The flight's delayed an hour and we won't be boarding for at least another 40 minutes. I smile at her urbanely. Internally I find myself howling at the moon.

Gdansk airport is nice. There's clearly been a bit of European money thrown at Polish airports. They're big and airy, chic and open to the skies. A coffee or a beer or a sandwich here, though probably expensive by local standards, is an absolute giveaway compared to the cheapest Wetherspoons back in Blighty. Really, what's not to like?

A taxi to my hotel would probably cost me little more than a fiver, but I'm still smarting from my Brussels fuck-up and I decide to take the local bus. If you go to Gdansk, please save yourself the bother and just grab a taxi – you are going to save so much money while you are here, you might as well. The bus takes me around grey insalubrious suburbs which remind me of Manchester in October and my heart sinks. It's a similar feeling to how I felt when I flew to beautiful Prague all those years ago then had to drive through its unloved communist environs on the way to one of the world's most awe-inspiring architectural jewels. In the end we were rewarded, but I have the same, 'Is this it?' terror. This is the Gdansk I imagined in my childhood. Yes, I was aware of it, and even back in Thatcher's ruined northeast, Gdansk evoked grim. A nice lad, who looks like Kirk from *Coronation Street*, wants to know what I'm doing in town; they're still getting used to tourists around these parts. He doesn't speak much English. But he's proof at least that not every young person has abandoned Poland. When we eventually reach the main station I stand up to get off, but he advises me gravely to stay on until the next stop. Once again, I make the wrong call, and as the bus drives a couple of miles to the next drop-off, my heart sinks. My phone is now dead so I have no idea where I am and I have no satnav. Oh God, what a day. I decide to look for either a bar, where I can recharge my phone, or a taxi. I walk for an hour, past overpasses and underpasses, motorways and empty classrooms, decay and strip clubs (closed). I'm in Poland and I can't find a bar. Oh, the irony. It's been a shit day.

This is also my fourth city in five days, more or less. I have four days in Gdansk. Time to take a breath. I'm reminded of my mother; every time we began a family holiday, there came a point, usually about 40 miles down the motorway to Scotland or, later when we pretended to be middle class, France, when my mother world take umbrage at my father's dreadful snappiness. She would, at this point, pronounce the holiday 'ruined' and demand the car be turned around back to Gateshead. A similar thing would generally happen on Christmas Days, when the festive season world be declared 'ruined' around 11.30 a.m. because of my dad's grumpiness, often real, often imagined. That's why I don't do organised jollity no more and I don't indulge in throwing dummies out of prams. It's especially futile when you're on your own... But if I was of that mindset, this is the point at which I'd be gearing up for an almighty sulk.

Miraculously, I turn a corner and find myself smack bang outside my hotel and opposite a river view which is at distinct odds to what I have encountered thus far. At last, some luck. And it's lovely. The Hotel Admiral is based just behind the Motlawa River, which gives the city its priceless outlet onto the Baltic Sea and cemented Gdansk's place as one of the greatest Hanseatic ports when this whole coastline of Pomerania was fought over by Prussians, Swedes, Poles and others. The hotel has a (not overdone) nautical theme, and it's a calm and peaceful spot from which to explore this fascinating corner of Europe.

I've checked the weather forecast for the remainder of my trip, and it's quite astonishing how I now seem to be following the clouds around Europe. The sun left Gdansk yesterday and will return, according to the forecasters, the afternoon after my departure. It's the same for all my remaining destinations. But here I guess it's appropriate. I remember Gdansk from the news. We were in the middle of our own miners' strike, and the Polish miners and ship builders were doing the same thing against a Soviet-installed, communist government they never asked for. The Cold War was at its apex and the world seemed to be caught in a perpetual October that is reflected in the city skyline this afternoon. Life seemed imbued with the feeling, like you get in October, that things were grim, and they were only going to get worse, and that we were a long time from spring. Total nuclear annihilation lay just around the corner. My dad shook his fist at the British miners on the news who he said were traitors to their country, but he applauded the same people striking in Poland. They were freedom fighters. Mrs Thatcher agreed. Frankie goes to Hollywood were warning about the whole European mess on their hit *Two Tribes* and the similarity between the moustachioed gay pop heroes of Frankie, Terry and Barry from *Brookside* and the freedom fighters from Gdansk and their leader Lech Walesa, was, well, striking – all permy men's hair, moustaches like shoe brushes and rustling shellsuits. At the time Lech and his colleagues also put me in mind of Freddie Mercury. It was reassuring, I'm sure, to many that in the gender-bending Eighties, there was still room for some old-fashioned real men like Walesa and Mercury.

Even looking in from Gateshead, the most depressing part of the most depressed place in the UK, Gdansk looked like a godawful hole. Grey, permanently sleeting, and riddled with communism and Catholicism, which seemed to teenage me just about the worst bargain made in history. I mean they didn't even have a Spud-U-Like. At least Gateshead had a Spud-U-Like. And there were rumours of things on giant spits called doner kebabs arriving across the river in glamorous Newcastle. One night my brother came back drunk from the Bigg Market with one of these aforementioned kebabs and he let me taste it. It smelled like, and had the consistency of, our Labrador Bruce's dog food Chappie. We pronounced it absolutely delicious. I felt sure that nobody in Gdansk was having a doner Chappie kebab and I was glad to be on the right side of the Iron Curtain.

There was absolutely no concept or consideration that Poland would ever escape communism's icy grasp back then, not just in our household but anywhere. I genuinely don't believe anybody saw it coming until maybe ten minutes before it happened and somebody somewhere said, 'You know what, they could actually pull this off.' And even then everybody else was like, 'Naaaah!' Gdansk, like Prague, Budapest, Sofia, Riga and Tallinn, was going to be entirely off bounds for the rest of my living days. I could only dream of how pretty those places sounded. But not Gdansk. Berlin Wall or not, this decaying post-industrial hellhole would never have featured then on my 'must visit' list. I didn't know much but I was pretty sure they didn't have Frankie Goes to Hollywood in Gdansk. Even ABBA, who were having a bit of an October moment themselves, wrote a song about how fucking depressing the world was, but especially around these parts, on the brilliantly moody and paranoid title track to their final album *The Visitors*. Nobody bought it. They wanted another *Take a Chance on Me* to cheer us all up. The whole world seemed depressed: mother, father, brother, sister, dog, ABBA. Seriously, thems were hard times. I don't think the young me would have known what to make of me being here today. I mean Prague, sure. Budapest, absolutely. But Gdansk? Not a chance. Yet here I am. And I'm glad I am.

So here's a quiz question. What does my first city Skopje have, that Thessaloniki and Gdansk don't have? Answer: a multi-ethnic identity. At opposite ends of the European continent, there is an invisible thread which connects the Greek and Polish metropolises. I hope it never stretches to funny old Skopje. A process, a way of thinking, which began in Thessaloniki one hundred years ago and reached its apotheosis here in lovely, smudgy-edged Gdansk in 1946, is still going on in Crimea, in the Donbass and in various corners of Asia and Africa.

The irony is that Skopje is known as a potential trouble spot precisely because it didn't take the awful steps pioneered across the Balkans and Asia Minor a century ago when the treaty of Lausanne allowed for the movement of millions of people out of their homes and the homes of their grandmothers and great grandmothers so that national boundaries reflected populations.

After World War II, the majority German city of Danzig/Gdansk was a ghost town. The German citizens, many of whom had invited ruin upon their homeland, and many other people's homelands too, were banished permanently as Poland was shifted westward to make room for a Soviet Union which was determined to have its territorial pound of flesh. The communist empire grabbed itself a nice slice of

East Prussia, the beautiful German city of Konigsberg, an enclave between Poland and Lithuania which that old dog Stalin surely knew would stoke trouble for the region for generations to come. Meanwhile Poland got the ruined husk of Danzig, a scarred beauty now surely doomed to eternal grief and ugliness. The temptation in ruined Danzig, now Polish Gdansk, among local communists, must have been to build over the past. But they didn't.

Danzig's beautiful Hanseatic Old Town, which was not so much rubble as dust, was rebuilt exactly as it had been depicted in paintings and photographs, save for a few Gothic script removals. The ravishingly handsome city I see before me is resolutely German in its architectural character, but now reborn by the incredible work of Polish artisans, who recreated the work of many hundreds of years, in just ten years. This was a massive act of love for a city whose 'liberation' by Nazi Germany presaged the destruction and enslavement of Poland by Germany and Russia. Again.

After World War I, one of the central promises of victorious Britain, France and America was the restoration of Poland, an ancient eastern bulwark between Russia and Germany, which had once held an empire which stretched from the Baltic to the Black Sea. But where was this Poland II to be placed? At the treaty of Versailles, Poland, which had largely liberated itself following the collapse of the three empires which had dismembered it, Germany, Russia and Austria-Hungary, was in a strong position.

Through victory in many post-Great War wars, Poland had carved itself a hefty chunk of land east and south of Germany. The only problem was that Prussian Germany, through years of military successes, sprawled along the southern Baltic shores, blocking access to a sea which the country felt it needed to cement its place as a significant port in the region and not be reliant on its powerful western neighbour. Most of the territory of West Prussia was handed to Poland, including the tiny seaport of Gdynia, which the Poles planned to turn into their own mini-Danzig. Meanwhile Danzig, a majority German city, was turned into a Free State, belonging to neither Poland nor Germany; thus Germany and Prussia, the cradle of German militarism, were sliced in two, East Prussia now adrift from its hinterland. Germans and Germany were thirsty for revenge and determined to return this city to its homeland.

After settling into my hotel, I go for a wander as dark falls over Gdansk. It really is strange to imagine anything bad happening here. By day and by night, the Old Town resembles a cityscape painted by Monet, all soft, gingerbread-house inviting. Some have objected to the way the city was restored, a remarkable act really by a skint communist country. They say that Germanic elements were rubbed out, but it's pretty obvious all around us. They say that perhaps walking around this beautiful town, it is too easy to forget the past. They say it's too perfect. But to me its restoration was simply an act of love and a raised middle finger to savagery and barbarism. A genuflect to the people who loved beauty, German, Polish and others, and who built this city in the first place. I hope one day the same thing will happen in Syria's Palmyra. Beauty must win.

I meet my guide Pieter at the hotel and he suggests taking me to a brew pub, a new thing in post-communist Poland. Poland has embraced capitalism and is good at it. Like their friends in the Baltic States, they are innate merchants and innovators. Everything works in Poland, and works well. It already feels a century ahead of Italy, not that Italy will give a toss. There's the same buzz of resurgence you get in Spain, so many years now since Franco departed. A delight and pride in a culture reborn. Sure there are international restaurants in Gdansk. But the majority do delicious Polish fare. And my God, it's good.

Before World War II, Poland's coastline was a teeny 140 kilometres; now it is 440 kilometres. The entire nation was shifted west to suit Stalin, who was unwilling to give up his gains from the evil Nazi-Soviet pact. Millions of Poles fled or were evicted from eastern territories handed to Belarus, Lithuania and Ukraine, and like the Smyrniots in Salonika, took the home of another evicted nationality, in this case the Germans. Consequently, Poland's west is actually its former east. Confused? You will be.

Pieter welcomes me to Gdansk, and we stroll the short 15 minutes to the brew pub on the other side of the Old Town. Poland has always been famous for its beers and vodkas but the country is currently in the grasp of a craft beer revolution, with microbreweries popping up all over the place. Most redolent of modern Poland is its conversion to cider drinking. At one point, cider sales accounted for only 1 per cent of total alcohol consumption, but sales tripled to 2 million litres in 2012. Things really took off when Poland fell out with Russia over its annexation of Ukrainian Crimea, followed by its barely disguised invasion of that country. The EU retaliated with economic sanctions and Putin hit back by cancelling imports of Polish apples, leaving the country, the world's biggest apple exporter, with mountains of unsold fruit. Not a country to be easily knocked back, Poland reinvented the old lemons/lemonade adage and 'if Putin gives you apples, make cider'. A social media campaign ensued; on Facebook 'Eat apples to annoy Putin' featured beautiful Poles happily, defiantly chomping into their rosy red and green orchard delights. Meanwhile the newspaper *Puls Biznesu* (literal translation: 'Business Pulse') ran an editorial entitled, 'Stand against Putin; eat apples, drink cider.'

Poland's mostly dessert apples aren't suitable for cider production. But a cottage industry sprang up which grabbed the attention of cider aficionados all over the world. Pieter chuckles as he tells me that Poles love to drink a toast to Putin as they sup from their new generation of apple drinks. This cheery defiance masks the true feelings of Poles about their gigantic neighbour to the north and east. While this nation is still prickly in its dealings with Germany to the west, things have improved considerably in recent years. But along with Estonia, Latvia and Lithuania, Poland considers itself most at risk from a revanchist Russia. Would the bourgeois West really risk a nuclear holocaust for, say, Latvia or Turkey? Putin thinks not, and Poles know only too well his dangerous game of brinkmanship has only just begun. 'Putin is a psychopath,' says one. 'But he is just one man.' 'Why is it still Russia? Always, always Russia causing the problems, inflicting the pain. Through all our lifetimes. Germany has grown up. Why can Russia never change? Why is it addicted to pain and domination?' For what it's worth, in my opinion, the gap of understanding between ordinary Russians and the rest of Europe needs to be bridged. Nations are not, and cannot be, inherently bad but sadly a few men and women are. But not many.

After saying goodbye to Pieter, I wander up Gdansk's main street as snowflakes begin to fall. It's time for dinner and I find a traditional Polish place where I sink into a happy, sleepy haze over a bowl of heartwarming *pierogi*. It seems that every country across the Eurasian landmass has its own version of the dumpling, from the British steak and kidney pudding to the Japanese *gyoza*. Poland's *pierogi* is a national classic which deserves a wider audience. My version tonight sits somewhere between a large open ravioli and a fried Chinese dumpling in shape and construction. It is filled with an earthy, shredded wild boar meat, resembling Cuban *ropa vieja*, flavoured with juniper berries, wearing a tender milky white dumpling dress, and drizzled with a whisky cream sauce and lots of ground black pepper. I've heard Polish food described as overly rich and heavy, but that's not my experience here. Like the saddle of doe with gingerbread sauce and grilled vegetables which I enjoy the following evening, Polish cuisine is a gastronomic cuddle and kiss on the head, an epicurean 'it's all gonna be alright' from the universe.

My heart suitably warmed, I find my soon-to-be favourite pub in town, The Red Light, a lovely bar of scarlet velvet and sinkable-into sofas that doles out hot chocolate, macchiato, the incredible local hazelnut schnapps, bison grass vodka and ingenious, lovingly prepared cocktails for a snip. Poland is a fabulous destination for many reasons, but prices here will win over any doubters. The most expensive dish on my restaurant menu, chateaubriand, comes in at £6. Local spirits, of an excellent quality, are about 40p a shot, while a Jaegermeister will set you back about 50p, a good coffee shot a few pence. What on earth are you doing over there when you could be over here? C'mon! Shake a leg!

The next day I go in search of the Kashubians. Nope, nothing to do with Kim and Kanye, these are a people inhabiting the area around

Gdansk, Pomerania and the former Polish corridor. Now I'm partial to an obscure national minority, but until I saw the sign proffering genuine Kashubian cuisine, I had never heard of the Kashubians. Naturally, I am like a rat up a drainpipe, and through the door of their folksy restaurant within seconds, ready for lunch. I can't give you much of an insight into the idiosyncrasies of Kashubian behaviour, but I can tell you their food is a delight. My starter of lard with bread and sweet and sour pickles would go down a storm in Hoxton, but you suspect the ladies here, in their colourfully embroidered pinnies, couldn't give a flying dill pickle what people with beards in east London think of them. Anyway, it's gorgeous. Grainy, light, crusty bread, salty butter, homemade pickles which crunch like Kashubian snow beneath the welly, and a deliriously moreish, bacony lard, flecked with ham, which tastes of pig x pig x pig. Yes, that's pig cubed. There's more pork in my next course of sauerkraut soup; more bacon, a thick, clear, carrot, onion and juniper broth with tangy sauerkraut, served inside a crunchy loaf of bread. In-bloody-genious. It's another grey day outside so I decide to stuff myself silly. Next course is pressed chicken roulade with salads and cabbage which I can barely find room for. With drinks and a tip I struggle to spend £10. The afternoon is earmarked for a bit of shopping. My trainers are falling apart, I've left behind a pair of Matalan's finest trousers in Thessaloniki, and despite my launderette day in Pisa, my wardrobe is ready for a bit of refreshment. I fancy something new to wear, to relieve the boredom which a low-cost airline trip wardrobe inevitably brings.

Finding my way to a snazzy mall I find a shop governed by a not at all naturally flame-haired temptress/bruiser, who shall be called Martika, and who gives new meaning to the term 'hard sell'.

No sooner have I picked up a shirt than I am physically shoved through a curtain and into a broom cupboard of a changing room and aggressively festooned with Polish shirts.

'Agh, *Polska*, *Polska*,' she trills. 'No China. No sheeeet... You Norvege? Very reech. Verry, verrrreee reech,' she continues without waiting for a response.

'Not Norvege,' I protest. 'English. Very, verrrreeee poor,' I tell her.

She feigns shock. 'No, *not* pooooor! Very, verreee reech!'

I try a shirt on which is way too big. It looks like a sack. Martika pushes her way into the changing room as I am disrobing.

'Ahhh! Sexeee! Sexeee! Sooooper sexeee!' she exclaims.

'Will you *please* leave me alone,' I say.

'Yes, yes! Soooooper sexy!' she says, well aware of my request but choosing to ignore me utterly. She returns to the shop and thrusts five more shirts through the curtains. I try another on and she barges in once again.

'Oooooooh! Wow wow wow! Looook man! Soooooper sexeee! Soooooper sexeee!' She motions at a woman passing the shop to come and take a look.

'Will you please stop it!' I say, snatching the curtains shut and throwing the shirts over the top rail. 'Leave me alone, you are crazy,' I shout over the curtains as I am hit by another deluge of shirts. I no longer care about etiquette.

'No *you* are kerazeeee!' she hoots, knowing she has identified today's victim.

I try a more fitted shirt and, God knows why, look at her for approval. She purses her mauve lips. 'No too fat. Fatteeee boom boom,' she laughs with delight.

'Well you can't frickin get enough of my good stuff,' I pointedly tell her. She throws another shirt at me. This one actually works, flattering my shoulders while disguising my, erm, fattee boom boom. I walk out of the shop with the shirt and three pairs of socks I didn't want but which she has thrown into my bag. I have lost the will to fight. '*You*,' I tell her as I walk out of the shop ten quid lighter, 'need to lay off the HRT.'

'Aagh yes,' she says smugly in the manner of one who knows the secrets of the universe. 'Sexeee, sexeee. Sooooper sexeee!'

Tsk. She's incorrigible, is our Martika.

The evenings are (bad play on words alert) very dgood in Gdansk. I'm told it's hopping in the summer months but I love its soporific, jazzy vibe. I spend my nights trotting around the cobbles, propping up cosy bars and inhaling *pierogi* in all their many delicious forms. After four nights, I am ready to move on, but I'm rested after my exertions in Rome and Brussels. Gdansk is not the place maybe for a mad adventure. But perhaps this city has had enough mad adventures to last lifetimes.

There are many alluring museums to visit here, but I opt for the tiny Museum of the Free City of Gdansk. There are no English translations, at least not on the day I visit, so I am left to draw my own conclusions through the many artefacts, newsreels, banners and bits of music. It's an eerily rewarding experience, reminiscent I guess of similar exhibitions for the more famous *Titanic*. But of course, the good ship Danzig was not a vessel but an entire self-contained world. Historical compromise turned it into one of Europe's last city states, but it seems the original Danzig Free City was much more of a success than its opponents liked to admit.

It was certainly not some failed bastard state. The remnants of life among the Germans who knew this as Danzig and the Poles who knew it as Gdansk and the Jews who just hoped to survive sends a shiver down the spine. This was not Syria in 2015, terrorised by some Dark Age philosophising. Danzig was one of the world's most advanced and 'respectable' cities. You could imagine the well-to-do populace, pushing their prams around these picturesque streets, stopping to gossip, listening to their gramophones and jazz from the US, drinking Coca Cola and washing in Pears soap. In some ways it looks idyllic as you examine the torn teddy bears and chipped rocking horses. But too many of these respectable people were seduced by the pull of Nazism. The Polish and Jewish populations were largely exterminated or worked to death; the Germans who weren't burned to death in their homes or bayoneted by Soviet troops were ethnically cleansed over another new border, as Germany was shrunk once again. *Feeling* – rather than just learning – for the first time what really happened here, it's hard to see the chocolate box town of Gdansk in the same light.

Afterwards I walk again to the peaceful water's edge where tourists take cruises on pirate ships and laugh and coo. It was here where the first shots of World War II were fired, a terrible legacy for any city. As I imagine the Allied planes strafing the water's edge, or the terrifying thudding and flashing the of the Luftwaffe bombing Polish positions on the edge of the city, I just thank God that this new generation of Gdanskers have again turned this town into a place of comfort, beauty and peace.

One last night in town, I turn a corner through a medieval alley and come upon about 40 German fraus in their sixties flashing their cameras at some monument or other; very probably the daughters of Danzig's former owners. I make like Madonna, raise my jacket collars and pull my hat down over my eyes.

'Pur-lease! No photograph! No pictures!' I cry scampering off, and they laugh as one. I've never made 40 elderly Germans laugh before, all in one go, and the incident keeps me amused for days.

At lunch the next day by the river, I tell my waitress that I'm leaving town today.

'Where to?' she enquires.

'Warsaw', I tell her.

She twists her lip and wrinkles her forehead with distaste. 'Ugh,' she says.

'You don't like?'

She puts a finger under her nose and raises it towards her forehead haughtily. 'Those people think they are so special. So pleased with themselves. And not friendly. Not like Gdansk.'

It makes me laugh, as a lapsed Geordie, and a former Mancunian adoptee, it could be my former neighbours talking about my home in the capital London. It's nice, and somewhat reassuring. No matter what setbacks your country may face, no matter how awful your rival may be, Scottish or French or German or Russian... It doesn't matter which country you are from, in Europe there is always an extra special loathing reserved for the residents of your capital city. I do love this continent of ours.

WHEREVER I LAY MY HAT...

While the remit of this book is to find you cheap flights, it doesn't hurt to help you save a bob or two on places to lay your spoiled head down for the night. Hopefully the advice below will be as useful to the budget traveller as the lover of luxury.

As I've already said, I'm a big fan of Lastminute.com's Top Secret Hotels. As soon as my booking was confirmed, I got confirmation of my hotel, the lovely Royal Court in Rome, which was exactly as described and where I had been promised. It may seem like a gamble, but you're guaranteed your whereabouts and accommodation of a certain standard. If, like me, you want a nice bolthole at a massively discounted rate, this can be your best bet, if you can wait to the, ahem, last minute to book. There's another nifty travel trick which will allow you to check if the website really is giving you the best deals out there. You have no need to wait to tap in your credit card details to find out the name of your hotel. Just copy and paste the description, and slap it into Google, encased in inverted commas. Then hit 'Enter'. There are multiple sites prepared to let the cat out of the bag, but Vakanz.club, a brilliant little blog, appears to be the most efficient. Using that trick you can discover that among Lastminute's Top Secret Hotels are the not-too-shabby Waldorf Astoria in New York and the divine Savoy in London. Once you know the identity of your hotel, check out the price for the same night on the hotel's own website, and then compare it against the best hotel booking websites (see below). If it's still ahead of the competition, you've got yourself a real bargain.

I thought I'd take a look at the biggest hotel booking websites. I've picked six of the most highly rated and popular sites. Three (Priceline.com, Hotels.com and Booking.com) are simple search engines; the others (Hotelscombined.com, Trivago and Tripadvisor) are meta search engines, which means they search the search engines. I searched for five different types of stay, all from 8th February 2016, and for one person.

SEVEN NIGHTS AT EL VIAJERO HOSTEL, CARTAGENA, COLOMBIA

Booking.com – **£101** in an 8 bed dorm **5/5**

Hotelscombined.com – same as above, but through Booking.com, so I'll knock off half a point for being less direct **4.5/5**

Trivago – same as above through Booking.com **4.5/5**

Tripadvisor – **£104 3/5**

Priceline – **£429.73** double with shared bathroom. Couldn't find dorm rate **1/5**

Hotels.com – couldn't find this hotel for those dates **0/5**

FOUR NIGHTS AT POD 51 HOTEL IN NEW YORK

Hotels.com – **£247** in taxes and fees **5/5**

Tripadvisor – **£247** with Expedia **4.5/5**

Trivago – **£247** with Hotels.com **4.5/5**

Hotelscombined – **£247** with Venere.com **4.5/5**

Priceline – **£301.80** (actually for a bunk bed room for two people, so a good deal, but once again failed to give us a price for a single traveller **2.5/5**

Booking.com – **£262**, at first glance the cheapest at **£219**, but their headline figure is misleading as it doesn't include taxes, and the rushed traveller could book this and then find himself lumbered with an extra **£40 charge**. Sneaky **0/5**

TWO NIGHTS AT GRAN CONDE DUQUE, MADRID

Tripadvisor – £85 with Agoda.com **5/5**

Hotelscombined – £86 with Agoda.com **4.5/5**

Trivago – £91 with Travelrepublic **3.5/5**

Priceline – **£98.60** – Arrgh Priceline, you still won't find me a cheap single room, but your double is only a few quid more so I'm giving you some extra marks **3.5/5**

Booking.com – £94 **2.5/5**

Hotels.com – £94 **2.5/5**

ONE NIGHT AT THE BOSCODO HOTEL, BUDAPEST

Trivago – £84 – single classic room *with breakfast!* **5/5**

Hotelscombined – £84 – single classic room *with breakfast!* **5/5**

Hotels.com – £88 – double no brekkie **3.5/5**

Booking.com – £88 – double no brekkie **3.5/5**

Tripadvisor – £88 – as above with Expedia **3/5**

Priceline – £89 – as above **2.5/5**

TWO NIGHTS AT ANY FIVE STAR HOTEL IN TALLINN, ESTONIA

Hotelscombined.com – £141, Radisson Blu Skyhotel with hoteltravel.com **5/5**

Booking.com – £146 Radisson Blu Skyhotel **4.5/5**

Trivago – £146 Radisson Blu Skyhotel through Booking.com **4/5**

Hotels.com – £165 Three Sisters Hotel with breakfast **3/5**

Tripadvisor – £166 Three Sisters Hotel with breakfast, through Amona **2.5/5**

Priceline – £194 Swissotel Tallinn **2/5**

And it's a clear win for Hotelscombined.com and for the meta search engines which take the top three places. If you only use one hotel search engine, on most occasions this baby is gonna get you the best deal. If you want one back up option, I'd go with Trivago. And if you're going upmarket, always have a gander at lastminute. com's Secret Hotels if they have them in your city.

1. Hotelscombined.com – **94%**
2. Trivago – **86%**
3. Tripadvisor – **72%**
4. Booking.com – **62%**
5. Hotels.com – **56%**
6. Priceline.com – **46%**

CHAPTER 9
STALIN'S GIFT

I loved Warsaw from the moment I set foot upon its soldier-flattened, bomb-shattered turf. Don't ask me why. It's just one of those tingles that you feel in your blood when you come face-to-face with the man/woman/city/beach/home/you-name-it of your dreams, something so good you never even dared imagine it. A feeling of coming home. I can't explain why. But by Jimminy I'm a gonna spend the next few pages doing my damnedest to try.

I had absolutely no expectations.

Most guides had painted the Polish capital as a post-communist, post-Nazi, post-beautiful architectural hellhole. It's not. I'm tingling even as I write this because I can't wait to go home to my new love. Sure, he's no beauty (and yeah, if cities have genders, then Warsaw is all man) but my God this hunk of turf is sexy. Gotham City meets heyday Manchester meets Brooklyn meets Krakow. Warsaw is a total ride. Just step inside and the Polish capital will do the rest.

I didn't make plans in Warsaw.

Warsaw had plans for me.

No wonder the rest of Poland can't stick Warsaw. Every non-Warsovian Pole I have met since my trip throws their hands up in horror at the very notion that I could find anything to admire in their ugly, arrogant capital. And sure, with pearls such as Gdansk, Wroclaw and Krakow, who on earth in their right mind would linger in the capital, a bewildering architectural basket case? Well, I would, but the 'right mind' qualifier admittedly might be a stretch.

The Krakovians find it particularly galling. Their city, they insist, is the true capital of Poland. One explains to me that liking Warsaw over Krakow is like preferring Glasgow to Edinburgh, or Berlin to Prague. Errrrm... and your point is?

Much of my Warsaw experience reminds me of my years in Manchester when I was a wet-behind-the-ears, 18-year-old, man-bobbed, travel and life virgin. Warsaw may be Poland's most cosmopolitan city, but that's not saying much, which is kinda similar to Manchester's relationship with the rest of the North back in 1987. Coming from Newcastle, England's second city, seemed impossibly exotic, but it was still relentlessly, rainily northern in character. Like Manchester back then, Warsaw just feels so completely unselfconscious. Lovely Wroclaw and Krakow worry if they are as pretty as fair ladies Prague or Vienna. Warsaw doesn't give a care. It knows it's *numero uno* in this neck of the woods. So our city of heroes does what it does. And quietly and surreptitiously it becomes Europe's best kept secret. I think if you are up for an adventure, and have found New York, Manchester or Berlin beguiling, then you will fall for Warsaw as I did. You never know what's gonna happen here. But you know it will be good and you know it's not up to you. Because everyone in Poland hates it, all the marketing budget goes on other parts of this fascinating country. Not having to jazz hand it like a *Strictly Come* dancer or engage in Mariah Carey style vocal histrionics like an *X Factor* contender leaves Warsaw free to just be itself. So there are no pirouettes here. If it were a band it would be The Smiths. Warsaw is uncompromising and aware of its own coolness, without being a twat about it. Gdansk is Prussian Poland, Krakow is Austrian Poland. Warsaw is Polish Poland.

It's little wonder that my first impressions of the city are good, mind. My £3.30 flight from Gdansk is short, easy and happy, almost entirely Polish, the entire half-full flight cheering with delight as we touch down in the capital. Do they know something I don't? I wondered. In the future, I will cheer when I land in Warsaw. A fairly long taxi ride sets me back just over a tenner and is easy as pie. I glide into my hotel, the swish 46-room H15 Boutique Apartments, am charmed by reception and led to my suite which is the price of some crumbling B&Bs in London. There's a real smooth buzz about this splendid city centre conversion, barely a year old, designed by Grzegorz Rygiel, who reimagined New York's Grand Central station. Its very location is enough to get a boy like me aflutter with excitement.

The clues are in the corners of the beautiful stucco columns which hold the ceilings proudly aloft: tiny hammer and sickles carved into the brickwork. The H15 resides in a former mansion block which the Soviet Union bought up in the 1920s and converted into their Moscow embassy in Warsaw. Stalin's mate Molotov spent time here and oh! the secrets these walls must breathe, not least the news that this nation was to be destroyed in 1939 thanks to a secret pact between former implacable foes, Hitler and Stalin.

History breathes through the corridors of this ravishing building, still decorated in the luxurious duck-egg blue chosen by its Soviet masters. The bedroom that I'll sleep in tonight was once more or less Stalin's personal turf in Poland, before he grabbed the whole country in 1945. It's a macabrely romantic thought. Christ knows what he'd think of my bedroom, which looks like it was something Madonna farted out of her womb in 1984, but it's so degenerate and bourgeois, and let's face it, camp, that I suspect he'd have suffered a double hernia and melted on the spot, just a slightly dodgy 'tache left atop a puddle of oozing bile. I do hope Warsaw's resurrection sees him spinning in hell somewhere. The room is amazing. It's post box red and white and black. Sexay! It's basically 1980s Athena brought back to life. My 18-year-old self would have sold a second cousin to white slavery to sleep in an Athena store. And that's what I'm doing tonight (no, the latter, not the former. I'm not *that* degenerate). At home it would be considered retro. But it's not retro in Poland because Poland never had Athena. They had communism, which officially banned highlighted hair, leather or denim jackets with tassels, permed mullets and Anthea Turner. The Polish equivalent of Athena in 1985 was a store painted dirty white, which sold itchy brown jumpers, soap in two colours, one broken glockenspiel, rusty tin can openers and grey tights that tore easily. That was communist reality. *We* had a hot man with a hairy chest holding a baby against his pecs. They had the Pope, General Jaruzelski and soft focus pictures of kittens on tins. IF they were lucky. It's a myth that Reagan and Thatcher won the Cold War. Andrew Ridgeley did. I spend at least an hour wowing at my accommodation, before eventually tearing myself away and heading out into a glistening Warsaw night.

It's midnight, and I've not had a really late night out since Thessaloniki. It's a Monday night too, so my expectation is a couple of drinks then back to Madge's pad. Warsaw, though, has other plans. There's a gay bar a couple of blocks away but I travel in hope rather than expectation.

I've heard stories about old skool east European homophobia in Poland, but if it exists in Warsaw, I certainly never encountered it, a giant playground of fun and ridiculousness that I don't reckon would hurt a fly. Truth be told, Poland has elected a new government since I left, the appalling Law and Justice Party. They're out for a fight with anyone apart from their pals in the Roman Catholic Church, their methods are anti-democratic, and they've already got sexual and racial minorities in their sights. Of *course* they have. They're big in the country. Of *course* they are. This is a country playing catch-up. Frozen in time for nearly 50 years, the warped machismo of Russian so-called socialism that was imposed on Poland, alongside a hand-wringingly anti-fun local Catholic Church, ensured that basically anyone who had a free spirit and a mind of their own, gay, straight, or otherwise, were persecuted in pre-free Poland. Unlikely bedfellows, the Catholic Church and the communist government might have loathed and feared each other but they were not averse to a bit of mutual masturbation when it came to homosexuality. You know the old saying, misery loves company. And you don't get much more miserable than communism and Catholicism. Except maybe the new government and the Catholic Church. Something tells me the libertarians of Warsaw will be having none of it.

Interestingly, the bar I head to, Lodi Dodi, named after a Snoop Dogg song, is right next to the police station. It is, as I expect, empty.

Apart from a smooching couple. They're about to close. 'Is there anywhere around here still going?' I ask the barman. 'We will tell you somewhere,' say the somewhat aesthetically mismatched duo, listening in, writing out an address. 'Take my number,' says the handsome, younger, half-French half-Tunisian part of the pair. 'In case you get lost.' How nice. They leave and ten minutes later I get a text. 'I want to be alone with you.' Oh crikey.

'What about your boyfriend?'

'He does his thing. I do mine.' Oh double crikey. It's been two and a half weeks and nobody has shared my bed. And this is a good bed. A designer bed made by Italians apparently. It would be rude not to, right? I satnav my way to the bar, but I can't find it so I text my new friend. I'm walking up and down a busy street. There is no sign of a bar at the address I've been given. Azire pops up out of nowhere, and beckons me to a gate with a buzzer. Then through to a concrete block, and into a lift going down about four levels from ground to a genuine bunker under the Warsaw earth.

And a kiss. A really, really nice kiss.

'Your boyfriend?' I ask.

'He will leave soon,' he tells me. We are not quite love's young dream. Did you ever have a holiday romance? It's an appealing thing, I think. Until about six years ago I had never had one. Not even with people I was romantically involved with. I mean, you can't have a holiday romance with someone you are involved with. It needs to be heady and intoxicating and boundless and ultimately doomed and futile to qualify as a holiday romance. I managed the whole doomed and futile bit on holiday with people I was involved with, but not the rest, sadly. I eventually had my first proper holiday romance in Sitges. I know. I didn't tell you about that when I was writing about Sitges. I told you about lancing my abscess instead. Well I couldn't, because I hadn't come out to you at that point. And I wasn't sure if we were ready. But I think we are now. Hold tight. So yeah, I had an actual real holiday romance in Sitges. A very handsome Welshman. He had a boyfriend and didn't want to cheat. I liked him so much I didn't want him to cheat. So we basically spent five nights taking long walks, patting each other sympathetically (heavy patting), brushing against each other and then apologising and talking far too much. He gave me his coat one day because I was dressed inappropriately for the weather (you can take the boy out of Newcastle…) and it was the loveliest thing anyone had ever done for me. I know. That last bit is terrible but true. On the last day, as we walked to the station, he slipped his hand in my hand. Bloody hell.

At 1 a.m. I enter this fantastic black-walled bunker full of Polish rockabilly lesbians, hotties, people so drunk they could barely pull off their break dancing moves to *Save a Prayer* by Duran Duran. By 3 a.m. I'm on the mic singing *Love on the Rocks* by Neil Diamond as his boyfriend heads off into the night. It's nice sharing my suite at Stalin's gaff with a friend, and he makes me feel more alive. We cranked up the tension during our hours together and Madonna, I feel, would be proud of our antics, Molotov impressed by the explosions. At 7 a.m. he leaves for his flight back to Luxembourg, and I collapse back to sleep for a couple of hours, smiling. Welcome to Warsaw.

I wouldn't normally bother getting up for breakfast after such a night, but I've arranged for a tour guide to take me around the city at 9.30 a.m. European hotel set breakfasts are funny affairs, either disappointingly arthritic versions of British or American ones, or nice but not extraordinary European offerings. Mostly my hotels have gone for the European variety, which is piles of hams, cheeses, pickles, cakes, fruits and yoghurts. They would be great for lunch, but at 9.30 a.m., with the option of another 30 minutes of kip, I have tended to pass. Obviously, if you're on a budget, that's crazy. A good brekkie can set you up until dinner time. But I usually enjoy lunch more than dinner in Europe, if I've skipped my morning munch.

A walk-in power shower plus that Warsaw buzz means I find surprising reserves of energy, and I'm glad I make it to the H15 breakfast, which alongside Sitges' Galeon was the greatest breakfast I ever beheld. Huge heaps of mixed oats were crammed into science lab bottles, and covered in thick, creamy yoghurt, wild berries and granola, thoroughly food fashion on point, but also thoroughly Polish and thoroughly delicious. It tastes like how you want the Polish forest winters to taste, woody and milky and crunchy and juicy and intermittently almost savoury. And then there are the hot sweet scones, someone doing incredible things with eggs, and the fattest, juiciest, saltiest, pickliest caperberries I have ever seen. I'm eating in a glass covered atrium which reminds me a bit of the cover of ABBA's *Voulez Vous*, shards of glass point up to the grey sky outside, and I'm settled into big seats like padded cells in moss green. My plate is filled with juicy cold cuts, smothered with piles of thick piquant grain mustard, made here. I've got fat slices of pork, beef and turkey and tubby tomatoes topped with vinaigrette and slivers of parmesan. I've piled this lot up alongside juicy pickled mushrooms and melting brie, and lots and lots of fresh ground coffee.

My guide and soon-to-become new friend Kuba arrives and we head off to visit the Palace of Culture and Science, also known as Stalin's Gift. Designed to be seen from every corner of Warsaw, a city he had systematically set out to destroy, its message was as plain as the moustache on Uncle Joe's face: 'You will never escape me.' It's as welcome as a love letter from your rapist. What a gift: like unwrapping a Tena Men from a close relative on Christmas day, Stalin's Gift was a wicked way to show disdain. Evil bastard, that Joe Stalin. It wasn't enough for him to see Warsaw flattened and Poland castrated. He needed absolutely to stand with his foot on the head of Russia's perceived enemy Poland, which had somehow ended the war on the winning side, and still been defeated. Sure, once Hitler invaded the USSR, Poland and Russia became cosmetically allied, at least. But there was no pretence. Russia had never accepted the independence of Poland as being in its strategic long-term interests.

So. there it stands today, Stalin's Gift, otherwise known variously as the elephant in lacy underwear, the Russian wedding cake and perhaps most aptly, Stalin's syringe. Deliciously bourgeois nightclubs, art galleries and cinemas took root. The Chippendales played in the same concert hall, in the late Eighties, as had been used by one Mick Jagger and the Rolling Stones during their Sixties heyday. Which is maybe not entirely progress. Perhaps in brighter, more hopeful days, the locals could look on this monstrous edifice wryly; a symbol of defeat by a bigger power, sure – but also proof that these things ain't over until they're over, and that the spirit of freedom will always beat the spirit of domination in the long run. Well, that was the hope until Putin came along and suddenly Poland's future began again to take on a familiar hue.

This 800-foot beast was meant to provide a taste of luxury and opulence to the masses when it was completed in 1955, after being thrown up into the sky in a mere three years. All gilded lifts, chandeliers and parquet flooring, it's again very Sixties Manchester in its interior, to the extent that it looks like a giant bingo hall on steroids, which of course is exactly what it is. It's less intimidating from the inside, more Elsie Tanner than communist mass-murderer. From the outside, my grandmother would have no doubt observed, it's all fur coat and no knickers. Well how could it be otherwise? Once they had paid for the fur coat, there was no money left for knickers. At times they've done their best to cheer up this sinister Voldemort's castle by painting it in different colours and featuring anything which might piss off Putin and might have Stalin spinning in his grave, which is admirable, like projecting onto it the colours of the Ukrainian flag when that country was attacked by the Russian president's thugs. Still, if you popped all of Skopje's bombastic buildings on top of one another, you still wouldn't get anything close to this architectural projection of Stalin's penis issues. There are few buildings I've ever encountered which exude such powerful projected malice. Some argue it's a warning from the past. I don't believe it should be gelignited. But could it be moved? I believe buildings like people exude energy, good and bad. I once felt physically ill after a week in the vicinity of Katie Price and Peter Andre. I'm sure this building must be doing the same thing to the people of Warsaw. You feel its creepy, clammy grasp wherever you go, which is pretty much exactly like spending time with Monsieur Andre. The least the locals deserve is an exorcism. And, hey, so does Katie Price, while we're on the subject.

The retro interiors have brought in Polish hipsters to the Palace of Culture's milk bar. Milk bars are the Polish equivalent of the British caff or the American drive-in food shack. One of the last remaining vestiges of life from the communist period, invented to provide sustenance of a dairy-based nature to a people starving on its feet, they are stereotypically filled with bitchy servers and customers so poor they used to chain the cutlery down. They survived long enough to come back into fashion for people on a nostalgia trip. The best ones in this city offer up huge helpings of doughty, doughy dumplings for a few pence. There's a windswept, forlorn quality to the one in the Palace of Science and Culture, like Lana del Rey should work there, sighing as she wipes down the plastic tablecloths. To be honest, the whole building is a Lana del Rey video transposed on to eastern Europe. Some of the younger generation here have learned to love that, and Stalin's Gift has become an unlikely ironic hero to many. We head in the lift to the viewing tower. The Palace was designed in socialist realist style, despite being inspired by the Empire State Building, by Stalin's favourite architect Lev Rudnev. Five thousand poor souls were drafted in from the rest of the communist empire and worked around the clock. There are 40 million bricks here and 3,288 rooms. We gaze across the jumbled skyline to a different world, Warsaw's still pretty Old Town. But this too, turns out to be a post-war construct. Stalin's pet project was rising out of ground that had been pummelled to ash. The destruction of Warsaw was visited upon Poland by both Nazis and Communists who, despite fighting each other bitterly since 1941, briefly and informally resurrected the Nazi-Soviet pact so that Warsaw's utter destruction was realised. Hitler, who already knew the Polish capital was destined to fall into Allied hands, went about the obliteration of all human, cultural and architectural life in Warsaw, for no reason other than utter hatred for the Jewish and Polish races. The Soviet Union, which allowed its Polish 'allies' to believe it was coming to relieve them following the Polish uprising, then stood at the east of the city and coldly watched as the Nazis took vengeance on Polish and Polish Jewish rebels. It was an act of pure mendacity.

There's an unreal quality to Warsaw's Old Town. From the Palace of Culture above, it appears to have been plonked like an antique tea-tray in the middle of Argos; it's lovely, but it feels artificial, like a film set, because it is. The Nazis took flamethrowers to Warsaw's libraries and museums, to absolutely break the will and spirit of the Polish nation. At the end of the war, there was so little left of Old Warsaw that when the Polish communist government decided to rebuild the shattered metropolis, all it had to base it upon was a couple of old paintings. So what you see in the Old Town, rococo tenements, a royal castle and a market square, is a replica, not a rebuilding. Nevertheless the new Old Town is a delight and we toast the future of eastern Europe's most dynamic and thrilling city with silky chocolate and marshmallows. You may ask yourself how a nation which was practically penniless after the war, with no Marshall Plan, managed to resurrect not just a few buildings but the entire architectural tissue of a ruined city. There were plans even to move the capital to Lodz and leave Warsaw as a gigantic war memorial. But before politicians could even debate such a move, Warsaw's extraordinary survivors began returning and began rebuilding the place by hand.

It would have been a huge blow to Poland and to the world to have lost this unshakeable city. In the end, Poland's now unchallenged capital, was rebuilt with the hearts and souls of the local populace as well as shovels and wheelbarrows. Their sacrifices were recognised in 1980 when UNESCO declared the Old Town a world heritage site. Proof that you can't keep a good man down, and definitely not my hero city, my new love, Warsaw.

It's time for more shenanigans, so with a Polish friend from London, Tomas, who is back home for the same few days, we plan a night of *pierogi* and karaoke. But first there is somewhere I am determined to drag him to, in the interests of, you understand, a good tale to tell.

I'm not sure if you are familiar with the concept of a gentlemen's sauna. Usually to be found in the gay listings, men's grooming, unblocking pores and generally getting clean, tend not to be the priorities here. 'Dating' apps have rendered such places practically redundant. In my experience, saunas usually end up like some depressing daisy chain of thwarted sex. Within ten minutes you are ranked on your scale of hotness, and you spend most of your evening being rejected by the men on the rungs above you while simultaneously rejecting those on the rungs below. This whole charade can go on for hours. So yeah, definitely not for me, thanks. Only Warsaw, being Warsaw, apparently does a bisexual version. That means that ladies also go along to partake in this game of conjugal snakes and ladders. I tell my friend. Though he fully expects it to be dirty and decrepit with just two old men gyrating in a whirlpool, I reckon you only live once. So off we go. At this point I must add that I am in no way, and have never claimed to be, bisexual, not even when, at the age of 27, I finally stopped pretending to like ladies. I know some people see labelling themselves as bisexual as a kind of safe house en route to full realisation of your desires. But I didn't have the energy for a second coming out. I like ladies, but not in *that* way. I do confess that I did have a strange twinge when my masseuse Natasha hugged me in Macedonia, but I didn't think it was a turning point. I was under the weather, emotionally vulnerable and feeling needy and she had very broad shoulders. That's all. OK?

We arrive at a building that looks neither dirty nor decrepit and me and my mate exchange glances. Inside I am confronted by a scene of such beauty my brain can't actually register it or take it in. I had a similar experience looking at Venice. It's like the galley scene from *Ben Hur*, plus all the most stupidly homoerotic bits from *300*, *Spartacus* and *Gladiator* welded together. If this is gay life in Warsaw, count me in. Except of course they aren't gay. They're bisexual. In one lounge room, there is indeed a real life female sauna goer. I don't quite know what to say, other than, her skin will be good tomorrow... you know, from all that sauna-ing and steam room-ing. Ahem. For the rest... I suspect this is the sauna's busiest night of the week because it allows them to walk into a room and take their clothes off without feeling entirely burdened by the weight of a label which carries with it so much, well, let's be honest, shit. That's a big hat to wear. A ten gallon one. I really hope, one day, people will just be able to nip in and nip out of life's experiences, without fearing they may accidentally be defined by them. A day later, I want to cry as I prepare to leave my beautiful Madonna suite en route to my ninth destination. There's a knock on the door, and I think it's to tell me to hurry up and check out, but actually it's to tell me to take as long as I like, and to hand me a 'present' of three delectable handmade chocolates. Warsaw, you're just too cute. Didn't I tell you, I would never be able to put this city's charm adequately into words? Aha!

As I jump into my cab to the airport, I'm back in Manchester in 1987, drawn by the gloomy romanticism of Morrissey, Living in Manchester was a happy accident. The Hacienda was just our local club. And then I remember reading some crap tabloid that said something about Manchester being the coolest city in the world. And suddenly we all got very excited and self-conscious. And of course, it immediately stopped being cool at that point. We were all just too aware of it. Warsaw is currently in the bit before it all goes tits up and pretentious. It's bloody amazing and has no idea how amazing it is, which is the sexiest thing of all. And I guarantee, at some point in the next couple of years, someone from *Vice* magazine will show up and declare it 'the new Berlin' or something naff like that. The kind of nonsense I would write.

LOOK BEFORE YOU LEAP

When perfecting your dream itinerary, and if you are cash conscious, it might seem preferable to grab the cheapest flight out of whichever city you were in on any given day, and see where your meanderings take you. Sometimes it can work. But the cheapest flight might not necessarily lead to the cheapest itinerary. For instance, a £3 flight is not such an amazing find if you're then stranded in a city with only one flight out a week, and that's back to the last place you left. Of course there are times when it can be worth doubling back on yourself, such as when looking for a cheap route into Mexico from Fort Lauderdale. But when booking that next airfare, it pays to have an idea of where you plan to head off to after that city, and maybe the one after that.

Meanwhile, always keep an eye on your route back home. If you're headed on a ten-city trek, as I was, you should thinking about routes back home by the time you've booked your seventh stop lest you inadvertently end up deep in the jungles of Madagascar and discover it's a three grand journey home via the Seychelles and Dubai. My flight from Brussels to Gdansk, for instance, was relatively expensive at £19 – but I knew that it would then take me into the universe of cheap Polish air fares (and cost of living). So my next two flights, to Warsaw and Wroclaw, were complete snips at £3.30. It's worth playing around with this. Often flights into Italy, for instance, are a tad higher than the budget airline average. But if you are happy to bob around Italy's less celebrated backwaters for a bit (and I certainly am), internal Italian flights can be a steal; with the same applying to Greece and Iberia, although to a lesser extent. Usually you will pay a bit more crossing national and continental boundaries, but if that takes you into a new budget market, then wahay!

That's not to say that you should book all your flights in one advance bundle. When I set off on my adventure across Europe, I had only booked my first four flights when I clambered on board my Wizz Air jet to Skopje. I had only a vague idea of where I wanted to go and where I would end up and that made the whole process more exciting and adventurous. The main reason for not booking all my flights in one go though, was because I knew I was going to be away for around a month, and I had worked out that flights in Europe tend to fall to their lowest level around 18 days before take-off. After that, although they fluctuate like a stock market, the trend does tend to be upwardly mobile. Similarly, flights booked in advance of 18 days tended to be more expensive; 18 days tended to give me the biggest array of cheap flight options. Of course, cost is not necessarily paramount. From most hub airports, there will be plenty of flights out of town for under £10, and the £2 difference in flying to, say, Brussels over Copenhagen is hardly going to be a factor in most people's choice of which city to plump for. More important will be whether they prefer *steak frites* and *moules* or foraged herbs and open sandwiches. Perhaps even more significant than that, though, is where you plan to go next and whether the range of choices floats your proverbial boat. Copenhagen is a great gateway to the Baltic and on to central Europe; Brussels is handy for Italy and Spain. You may have heard about Spain's pristine and, at one point utterly unused multi-million-euro Castellon Airport, prettily perched among the Costas.

It's cheap as sangria to get to, but you can only really fly back to Stansted. Likewise, out of season Rabat, La Rochelle (indeed many French airports) and Linz in Austria offer limited follow-on options. Geography, of course, also plays a part: airports on Europe's edges such as northern Norway, western Iberia or far flung Greek islands won't offer as many connections. I chose to go to Thessaloniki, knowing that it was a bit of a cul de sac, because it was a city I had always wanted to see, but it's likely your route out will take you via Athens or Rome – though that's no great hardship.

Hunt out the hidden gems. Strasbourg provides an unexpected gateway to Bosnia and vice versa; Italy to Transylvania. Skopje may seem an obscure choice, but links with Barcelona as well as Luton bring it firmly within the European adventure mainstream. For me, the most interesting and successful trip would balance out your famous hubs with your hidden gems. In travel, as in life, always be thinking a couple of steps ahead. Madrid, Brussels, Dublin, Paris, Copenhagen and Oslo are good stops en route to Britain, as are Poland, Latvia and Lithuania thanks to the EU open labour market. It's hard to come by a definitive list of the world's top travel hubs. There are many ways to measure it, and airports with the most traffic, are not necessarily the most use for the purposes of this book. Heathrow in London is a giant, Stansted a dwarf, in terms of travel footfall. But if you're seeking a cheap adventure with flights under a tenner, it's far more likely that you will be setting off from or travelling through the Essex portal than the west of London transport colossus. Here's a list of what I reckon are the world's most useful transport hubs. If you're wondering how to get home, one of these hubs will likely ease you cheaply back to where you need to be.

TRAVEL HUBS

NORTH AMERICA

1. Fort Lauderdale
2. New York City
3. Los Angeles
4. Miami
5. Toronto
6. Chicago
7. Boston
8. Dallas
9. Panama City
10. Cancun
11. Mexico City
12. Houston

EUROPE

1. London
2. Dublin
3. Barcelona
4. Madrid
5. Copenhagen
6. Frankfurt
7. Rome
8. Alicante
9. Milan
10. Lisbon
11. Oslo
12. Warsaw

AFRICA

1. Johannesburg
2. Sharm el Sheikh
3. Lagos
4. Cairo
5. Cape Town
6. Nairobi
7. Marrakech
8. Fez
9. Accra
10. Mauritius
11. Hurghada
12. Tunis

ASIA

1. Delhi
2. Dubai
3. Mumbai
4. Tokyo
5. Beijing
6. Shanghai
7. Seoul
8. Colombo
9. Islamabad
10. Hong Kong
11. Chennai
12. Bengaluru

OCEANIA

1. Melbourne
2. Sydney
3. Nourmea
4. Auckland
5. Adelaide
6. Brisbane
7. Perth
8. Christchurch
9. Cairns
10. Gold Coast

SOUTH AMERICA

1. Bogota
2. Sao Paolo
3. Buenos Aires
4. Rio de Janeiro
5. Cartagena
6. Santiago
7. Lima
8. Quito
9. Caracas
10. Montevideo
11. Brasilia
12. Belo Horizonte

SOUTHEAST ASIA

1. Kuala Lumpur
2. Bangkok
3. Hong Kong
4. Singapore
5. Bali
6. Manila
7. Phuket
8. Ho Chi Minh City
9. Hanoi
10. Koh Samui
11. Chiang Mai
12. Yangon

Outside Europe, the USA, Canada and Mexico, options for low-cost travel are mostly limited to Brazil and Colombia in South America, parts of the Indian subcontinent, South Africa and southeast Asia.

HIDDEN GEMS

Some you will have heard of, some not. Some may be heaven to you, others hell, but here is my completely subjective choice of ten destinations to look out for if you're touring Europe or North America. They've been chosen because of convenience, location, accessibility, affordability, culture and that adventure factor which I think would make them a fascinating addition to any multi-stop trip. I've left out all of the cities I've travelled to in this book. Basically, these are the places I would be smugly swerving Paris and Miami to enjoy.

EUROPE

1. Lviv
2. Perugia
3. Valencia
4. Kosice
5. Nuremberg
6. Figari
7. Bucharest
8. Catania
9. Vilnius
10. Tulsa

NORTH AMERICA

1. Fort Lauderdale
2. San Antonio
3. Oaxaca
4. Richmond
5. Long Beach
6. Nashville
7. Myrtle Beach
8. Albuquerque
9. Providence
10. West Palm Beach

CHAPTER 10
BETWEEN A WROC
& A HARD PLACE

It's not easy, this gallivanting all over Europe malarkey, you know. I may come across as an ungrateful pleb in saying this, but there were times on my schlep around some of Europe's most cultured and beautiful cities when I just couldn't be bothered. I wanted to be at home with the papers. 'Please take away this gourmet Polish/Catalan/Belgian fayre. I want chips with curry sauce, or cottage pie or a proper traditional English curry. Less of this foreign muck!'

Obviously, I'm exaggerating a little, but there were times when I suffered on your behalf. Sitting in rainy Leytonstone in December, I'd kill to be back in breezy, happy Thessaloniki or even freezing cold Brussels, at least for one night. It was an incredible adventure and one I plan to repeat, but you really could go nuts and fly home after nine days.

The good news is that you never get bored, because you are always a short hop from your next destination. This leaves less time for introspection, if you're travelling alone, or for rowing, if you are prone to making lists of the annoying personality foibles of your travel companion. You see, a month on the road is hard. Don't believe anyone who tells you it's not. Frankly, I don't know how Fleetwood Mac do it. I was banjaxed on many occasions, and I didn't even have to get up and sing *Little Lies* and *Gypsy* every night to millions of adoring fans (although I'm quite sure I would be *amazing*!).

Travel, over a certain number of days, is hard for the same reasons that Christmas is hard. I've only really become any good at either in the last few years. And that only came about as I began to understand the nature of my travelling companion: a moody, anti-social, extrovert introvert with a tendency to overthink himself into a state of wild screaming panic or deathly inertia, i.e. me. There have been times when I've been away when I just wanted to lock myself up in my hotel because I was scared to go out. Scared of what, I hear you ask? Absolutely nothing and absolutely everything. Have you ever been overtaken by the fear?

By and large, I find Christmas to be a complete pain in the posterior. Closely followed by New Year. By the time they come around, people have been whipped up into such a frenzy of this-has-gotta-be-the-best-everness that all it takes is a faulty tree light to ignite an Archduke Franz Ferdinand-type chain of events which ends up with one person shouting, 'I never did like your mum anyway, her breath smells of rotting onions, her so-called homemade sausage rolls are from Iceland, cos I saw the box, the crafty cow, and her sexy Santa outfit last year nearly made me bring back my festive pickled egg.' And the other person retorting, 'Well your dad didn't seem to mind when I caught him helping himself to her chicken vol-au-vents in the kitchen while you were passed out like a lush in front of the Queen's Speech.'

The idea of organised jollity, that everybody should be in exactly the same mood on the same day, is not only absurd but also pretty nausea-inducing. I have an inherent inability to fake my moods. It's knowing that I don't have to which keeps me largely content and calm and easy to be around. I would say that I'm nice company by and large. But I can't and won't pretend to be happy when I'm feeling sad. Not for anybody. Cos that's where madness lies. And trust me I've been there. If you go travelling for a month, nothing will ever run completely smoothly, you will make mistakes, things will go wrong. You will have days when the sun is shining and you will still feel like shit. That's life. The clouds won't move until you acknowledge and accept their presence.

And meanwhile I'm on my seventh consecutive literally cloudy day as I arrive in Wroclaw and it's not predicted to move anywhere soon. I need daylight, proper daylight. I've not seen the sun in over a week and it's starting to do my head in. I feel bad for Wroclaw, because it's an incredibly pretty place, but I can't take it in. I'm having one of my bad days. I can't fight it until I see sunlight I decide. Poor Wroclaw could suffer the same fate as Pisa; overshadowed by my rotten mood.

I'm staying at Wroclaw's Hotel Patio, bang in the centre of town, just off the main square. The Hotel Patio is kind of a retort to the H15 in Warsaw. Whereas the rooms in the latter appear to be an homage to an Eighties consumerist past which never actually happened here, then the Patio's rooms evoke real Polish hotels back in the early Eighties, but without the dust or the listening devices. There's a lot of something which resembles chipboard and a melange of brown patterned wallpaper. It's a Scandic hotel, so it's a bit like one of those noir dramas; I think, but I'm not sure, it's been designed to be somewhat brutalist in appearance. After the Hubba-Bubba, Cherry Lips, Monster-Munch, Cola Bottle sugar rush of the H15 suite, it is something of a slap around the face with a dead wet haddock but I can see that this reaction may well be a symptom of me not having seen daylight since Rome. I stare at the edgy chipboard and the Eighties office stationery metallic bin and it evokes memories of my first student residence. This should be a happy thought, but tonight it evokes ripples of feelings of my first broken heart. I think perhaps it may appeal more to people who never lived through the woodchip years. It's got rave reviews pretty much everywhere. On Trip Advisor Barry M enthused: 'Rooms were all good, modern & clean. Twin rooms had plenty of space for friends sharing.' Another fan was Ivan L, who whooped: 'The rooms are cosy and clean, with nice modern furniture and comfortable beds, and all necessary facilities.'

So don't take my word for it. It's got a soft bed and a roof, so how can I be so ungrateful? Anyway, it's nothing that won't be sorted by a short, 20-minute sobbing session, morphing into a ten-minute existential, bone-deep, animalistic howl. Then a five-minute quiet, high pitched wailing as my head is buried into the itchy, brown-patterned bedding. There, that's better. At the end of my emotional outpouring, I'm like a child weeping when it's been sent to bed at the end of its fifth birthday party, and has cried so hard it has no idea what it was crying for in the first place. What *was* I crying for again? Ah, that was it. All gentle souls drowning in life's grief, mate. That and the chipboard.

I don't *really* think the chipboard is the reason for my emotional state, more a catalyst. I'm tired, my serotonin levels have hit rock bottom due to the lack of light (I couldn't survive in one of the Scandi-noir dramas; I need light, and lots of it). And I've managed nearly 25 days on my own. That can be tough even on the hardiest soul. Don't get me wrong, I love my own company. Never needing to compromise, always doing what *I* want, only having to deal with my own stupid moods, not needing to feel guilty if I'm feeling anti-social. I very rarely feel lonely. But perhaps now, and it's painful to admit, I am feeling a little alone. I need a cuddle. And I don't mean of the Warsaw kind. There are two kinds of cuddles. Well, there are if you a man. Ooh cuddles, them's dangerous things. Intoxicating and addictive. There are millions of people around the world having ill-advised or just slightly unsatisfactory sex right now as we speak, when all they really wanted was a cuddle. But sex is easier to get, don't you know. If you ask someone for sex and they don't want it, they at least feel flattered that you wanted to have sex with them. If you ask someone for a cuddle they not only think you are weird but are also offended that you have specifically insisted that you don't want sex with them under any circumstances. There are people locked in wholly unsuitable marriages and relationships because they became addicted to on-tap spooning. There are adults who should never have been permitted to have kids, with messed up offspring who go out and commit mass murder because mummy only really wanted the cuddles she didn't get from daddy any longer. Cuddles ruin lives and break hearts. I'll let you into a secret. I once spent three hours in bed, fully clothed, cuddling a total stranger who spoke no English. It was on his instigation and I couldn't think of a good reason to say no, because at the time I was feeling in need of one myself. At the end he left and that was that. It was an entirely happy and mutually rewarding experience. It was calm and loving because it came with no baggage, guilt or expectations, just a mutual understanding that we needed this and were exchanging kind and caring energy.

Oh dear, I seem to be digressing on my digressions. But do not underestimate the power of loneliness on your travels, and even more importantly, don't give yourself a hard time for feeling it, if you do. I always feel like a bit of a failure when the lonely bug bites but I know I've chosen to sail this ship alone. There's a lot to think about, catching 11 flights in one month, arranging accommodation, arranging what to see. Just not forgetting your passport 11 times can be tiring. At home, if something goes wrong, like you lose your keys, or your wallet is stolen, or whatever, there is always someone you can fall back on. Or even if you're just feeling a bit crap and just want to opt out of responsibility for your life for a day; we all have someone who will take charge and pet us a bit until we're feeling better. But on my journey, 25 days of only relying on me, and not being sure if I'm even responsible enough, is cumulatively wearing. I think that's the nub of my pain.

So it's all these things and nothing. I think sometimes we invent reasons to cry. I think we even subconsciously create drama or rows so we can let go of the emotion. Women cry a lot which I am pretty sure is why they live longer than men. I once took anti-depressants, and didn't cry for four years. I felt absolutely wretched. When I finally came off them I cried a Niagara of tears in the middle of Islington High Street over absolutely nothing and absolutely everything. A concerned couple stopped to offer help and were somewhat confused when I replied, between snotty sobs: 'No... It feels... [sniff] ... really nice.' Of course as men, we are taught *not* to cry (although I do see that changing a bit with the young uns, thank God). I cried at neither of my parents' funerals because I couldn't physically do it in front of people, but broke down in tumultuous raindrops of grief while watching an episode of *Home and Away* where some blonde was declared blinded for life. To put this in context, I never followed *Home and Away*. I didn't know who the bloody hell she was, and I understood enough about the world of soaps to realise she would be right as rain within a month after a miracle bump on the head with a tin of beans. Oh, and I knew it wasn't real. But I just had to let those chemicals out, and to feel that pain which, like joy, is just a natural part of being alive. You can't have day without night. When people watch *Beaches* and sob and wail, they're not crying because they actually think Barbara Hershey is dying before their very eyes. They're expressing a grief buried so deep they very probably don't even know what it is. It's good. It keeps us sane. Ish. I leave the hotel more because I want to get out of my room than because I feel up for going out. This is very unlike me. I love the buzz of a new city and this is no reflection on Wroclaw. I'm actually suffering from travel fatigue which is very annoying and very First World, but there you go. I'm the kid who ate too many sweeties and is now retching over a Mars Bar. Over a bowl of excellent but not really appreciated wild mushroom soup I ponder the nonsense of the saying, 'The last mile is the hardest mile.' Nah. That's where you get your second wind. It's the second-last mile which is the killer. I decide to start afresh the next day.

For reasons that are not immediately obvious to anyone around these parts, Prague and Budapest became the star cities of the newly liberated central Europe. After that came Poland's most famous medieval jewel Krakow. Wroclaw, perhaps because it's as unpronounceable to Brits as Edinburgh is to Americans (it's pronounced Vish-lav) barely merited a mention, yet it's as beguiling a place as any around these parts. A short nosy around the city, which is one of the two 2016 European Capitals of Culture, and its sites perhaps offers a clue as to why Wroclaw was so backward in coming forward. This city's myriad pretty gables, fountains and spires, hide a past as dark as any in central Europe. A poke around this daintily charming university town reveals stories that bring yet more dishonour upon this continent, and reveal a tale that really doesn't leave any nation basking in glory. Walking around a place of such beauty it is hard to understand that it could be home to such acts of barbarity as Wroclaw witnessed. Or as it was known then, the 'model' Nazi city of Breslau.

Breslau was the capital of German Silesia, a part of Prussia which had been held by Poland and Bohemia at times in its history, but had been resolutely Germanic since 1526. It had last been part of Poland in 1202, so the post-war notion, propagated by the communist government, that Wroclaw was a 'recovered territory' which had been waiting to return to the Polish motherland, was probably even more fanciful than England demanding reunification with France's Aquitaine after 600 years. Unlike Danzig there was only a negligible minority of Poles in the city, though it held in its walls many thousands of Jews. Breslau was turquoise and honey and pink and pretty. A centre of culture but also, after the calamity of World

War I, a hotbed of resentment. Its city walls were now filled with Germans who fled the successor states of the German and Austrian empires, especially those from Poland. Poland had been granted a big chunk of formerly German territory in Silesia and to suddenly be the underdog to the uncultured, uncivilized (so they thought) Poles, was too much for many Germans to bear. Embittered and demanding revenge, they moved west across the border to the safe house of resolutely German Breslau. The city was already a Prussian stronghold and proud bastion of German nationalism. Breslau was ripe, even before this influx, for seduction by Nazi lunatics.

At the pivotal 1933 elections, a staggering 200,000 of Breslau's citizens voted for Hitler's NSDAP party. It was to be one of the largest mass-suicide notes in history. For Jews, Poles, socialists and other undesirables, years of terror were to ensue, but the city's German population did better than most in the Reich, out of range of bombers until the war's last gasps. But not all German nationals were seduced though.

My incredible, amazing and brave German-Russian friend, Phillip, told me just one story – there were many others – about a pastor and theologian born in Breslau who was executed by the Nazis in 1945. He was a member of the German resistance. We weren't taught about him in Britain but he gave his life fighting those monsters. He was stripped naked and hung by wire with his co-conspirators. His name was Dietrich Bonhoeffer and he wrote:

'Silence in the face of evil is itself evil: God will not hold us guiltless. Not to speak is to speak. Not to act is to act.'

As the Soviet army battled its way back through Poland, it became clear to all in the city that a day of reckoning would soon descend upon Breslau. In August 1944, Hitler declared Breslau was to be a closed military fortress and defended at all costs. Most of the civilian population were trapped in the city, and Governor Karl Hanke, a personal favourite of Hitler, ordered execution squads onto the city's streets to shoot dead any civilian showing signs of defeatism. The defence of Breslau was a futile and militarily useless undertaking which underlined more than anything the Nazi contempt for the lives of its own civilians. In January 1945 Breslau's Deputy Mayor Wolfgang Spielhagen was publicly shot, his body thrown in the River Oder as a warning to others who criticised the plan. Hanke stubbornly refused to allow the evacuation of civilians from Breslau until 19th January, by which time most of the transport networks out of the city had been destroyed by Russian shells. Children were stampeded to death at the train station, and many people decided to make their way out of Breslau on foot. As temperatures dropped to around −15°C, 100,000 citizens, mostly women and children, froze to death attempting to make their escape. An 80-day siege ensued, the city eventually surrendering two days before Germany accepted utter defeat. The siege cost the lives of 170,000 Breslau residents, 6,000 German and 7,000 Soviet troops, and had achieved nothing. Between 80 and 90 per cent of Breslau was damaged with around 70 per cent of it utterly ruined. Three quarters of the damage was attributed directly to the self-destructive policies which the German military took to prevent the city falling into Soviet hands.

For the remaining population of Breslau the nightmare was not yet over. Drunk and angry Soviet troops, determined to avenge the German atrocities in the east, went on a rampage of murder and rape. The post-World War II Potsdam Conference lacked even the misguided or fake morality of the post-World War I knees-ups to divvy up the spoils of war. Stalin had absolutely no intention of handing back his share of the booty from the bestial Nazi-Soviet pact. Estonia, Lithuania and Latvia remained occupied nations, even as the USSR dubbed them joyously enthusiastic new member states. Meanwhile a massive eastern chunk of Poland was grafted on to the western Soviet republics of Ukraine, Belarus and now Lithuania, which got it's fiercely contested capital Vilnius/Wilno back from Poland.

At Potsdam, stuck with the fact that the Soviets would never hand back an inch of territory stolen in the east, the Allies agreed that Poland would be put on wheels and moved east to the Oder-Neisse line. In return for being forced to accept the loss of 116,000 square miles of land in the east, Poland was handed Danzig, Breslau, Silesia and the lower half of former East Prussia plus everywhere else east of the rivers, a territory totalling 70,000 square miles of turf. As 14 million people were forcibly uprooted, Europe's geography was changed forever. Germany and Poland finally became (mostly) nation states. And though firmly chained to the new Russian empire at that point, Poland's new geographical reality perhaps did make it easier for the country to make the transition to the EU when the communist sandcastle eventually blew over.

Refugees, many from the east, arrived in the newly renamed city of Wroclaw, a devastated place which had been sold to them as a bright new start. Wroclaw rose again, but the new Polish masters obliterated most Gothic, Germanic and Prussian styles from their architectural palette, even more than in Gdansk. The city that was destroyed by Nazi hands in 1945 was rebuilt by Polish ones over the next 20 years, leaving no doubt that this new old city belongs within its new family. Now it has a gentle, Bohemian, perhaps even Baroque or Hapsburg (they did once rule here) feel to it – though your guess is as good as mine as to what is *real* history and what is historic confection. With its sparkling rivers, 12 islands and 120 bridges, Wroclaw has a dreamy feel. It is beautiful, moving and captivating, but there's something perhaps a little too perfect about the re-born cultural metropolis. Yes, even if I didn't know its history, I would have to confess, it feels unreal.

Once there was a quiet shame among residents about how they came to live here. Many of the new denizens of Wroclaw had been roughly thrown out of their own homes by Soviet forces in the east, particularly those who came here from Lvov (now Ukrainian Lviv). The dispossessed had become the cuckoos in someone else's nest. But with freedom came an acceptance and an embracing of the past that has allowed the city to no longer feel embarrassed to take centre stage again. It is the fastest growing city in Europe's fastest growing country.

Now, while problems between Russia and Poland are at their worst since 1945, a kind of reconciliation between Poland and Germany has taken place here on the streets of Wroclaw, which are thronged by German tourists. So too with the Jewish faith; the beautiful White Stork Synagogue, left to rot after the war, has been restored and reopened.

The sun has finally begun to poke out after a week of eluding me and I spend the day getting happily lost among the city's illustrious piles. The buildings are as pristine as Skopje's ancient monuments, here prettily painted in pastel blues, pinks, green and orange. Every now and then you get a glimmer of old Prussian Gothic, as at the imposing Old Town Hall, but mostly the style is sweet Baroque. Maybe after the harshness of the war, the new citizens wanted something a little gentler – but more likely, the people who re-imagined this town brought with them the old Austro-Hungarian Hapsburg style from Lvov and Krakow. As you wander, be careful you don't fall flat on your face tripping over a dwarf. There are over 300 dwarf statues scattered around this city – adding yet more sweetness. It may seem like pure whimsy but Wroclaw's dwarfs are the symbol of the Orange Alternative – a dissident group from the communist era, who played their part in bringing this city back to its rightful place in the heart of Europe.

For dinner I want to taste the genuine local cuisine, so it makes sense to eat in Karczma Lwowska, a restaurant serving the cuisine of Lwow/Lviv some 604 kilometres to the east. Situated on the main square, this is an incredibly handsome and ornate place to dine, resonant of the old east, the Polish lands which are no longer Polish. The food is as rich and melodious as the place itself, thick leather and wooden beams, and I feast on roast pork stuffed with plums and served with hot horseradish, followed by 'Leopolitan' veal in a honey and lemon sauce and finally Galician poppy seed cake with chocolate sauce. It's great that old Polish Lvov lives on in Breslau, but I wonder where in Germany you can find Breslau cuisine. Anyway, the whole delicious thing sets me back £14. Happy days.

I have an evening flight to catch to my next destination from Wroclaw airport. I feel like I should have done and seen and experienced more here. I mean, this is an incredible slice of Europe. So I'm afraid I let you down. Like Pisa and my teeth, Wroclaw and my mind had 'issues' to deal with. I will come back. In a city of ironies, the airport presents the icing on the cake, built by Hitler in 1938 on firmly German turf in preparation for the obliteration of Poland. There's something spooky about Wroclaw Copernicus airport, as I think perhaps there is about the whole city, but I will have to come back to check out if it was just my serotonin levels going wild.

Flying around Europe's lesser known airports has generally been an absolute pleasure, but this place is disconcerting. It's not so much the Hitler link, as the fact that I have this whole beautiful, modern airport to myself. As I waltz through security I start to take pictures of this cavernous empty space until about 12 security staff start running towards me. Oops. Well I'm sure they were glad to be given something to do. It's my last hour in Poland and I celebrate with a greedy buffet of airport food and drinks. It's SO flipping cheap and I want to get my money's worth before I land in Scandinavia. Ahhhh. It's the last leg. And I'm on my last legs.

A HAND-HELD WALK THROUGH THE PROCESS

I will now walk you through a couple of scenarios of how to grab these surely cheaper-than-cost flight bargains, with the simplest one first. On my European trip I booked more than half of my flights when I was already on my jaunt, but for the purposes of this lesson, I'm going to pretend to book beforehand. Obviously, there are as many scenarios as there are travellers, this is just intended to show you how to use the methods you have learned in this book; and you might pick up some handy tips on cheap routes into the bargain. Have fun playing with itineraries, that's the best way to learn...

SCENARIO ONE

DAVID: *I want an adventure so take me anywhere so long as it's stupidly cheap. I can go anytime in the first half of this year from London. Just keep getting me the cheapest flights and I want six or seven stops before I fly back to an airport in the south east. I want three nights in each city. No late night arrivals (after 8.30 p.m.) and no flights leaving before 8.30 a.m. because I like to party late and I don't want expensive taxis to the airport. I don't want more than two stops in the same country.*

OK, this is nice and simple. Three nights in every location means he will be flying on busy days of the week as well as cheap ones, but if he's taking the cheapest flight, we should still get some amazing deals.

The main danger is that he's not looking where he is going so we could end up, after six or seven stops, in a city which costs a bomb to return from, but let's get weaving.

To begin, we need to search the next five months to find the cheapest flight out of London to anywhere. I start with Skyscanner.

FROM:	London
TO:	*leave blank or click on* **Everywhere**

Be sure to tick the one-way button, and uncheck the direct flights button.

DEPART:	*and click on* **Whole Month**. *When you get the list of months, select* **Cheapest Month.**

Skyscanner should now, in theory, find you the cheapest flight leaving London in the next 12 months, as prices stand at that moment. In half an hour it could be different. Remember to select how many people will be travelling. If you are in a group or couple, check the cost of buying tickets individually as opposed to as a two or a three. If the airline had two seats for £10 and the next seat is £20, you will all be charged the higher rate if you buy as a trio. So you would end up paying £60 instead of £40. Now the exciting bit, hit Search.

Skyscanner finds me a flight to Basel in Switzerland for £6 in February. But when I go to book it, it's shot up to £9.99. That's still cheap, but it's a 66 per cent hike. I move on to the next cheapest city, Szczecin in Poland, which is £7, but again shoots up to just short of a tenner. There are actually scores of flights for under £9.99, but they all shoot up to that magical figure when I attempt to book. There's definitely something a little fishy going on here.

It turns out I've picked a strange day to do this search. A teen blogger has discovered it's cheaper to fly from Sheffield to Essex via Berlin than to catch the train. The story has gone viral. It seems like a big coincidence that Ryanair has rounded up the cost of a ton of its cheapest flights on the same day. I know that the airline is touchy about the subject because I have asked them for information previously. Who knows? Most importantly, the cheap flights from other European cities are still there. I'm left with a smorgasbord of ten pound flights from London for David. Before I stick a pin in a map, I decide to see what's occurring on Kiwi.com.

Going over the first six months of the year, it finds me only one flight under £10, to Szczecin in Poland with Wizz Air. This is a non-starter, because I know the only flight out of town three days after I land is to a former Norwegian whaling station named Sandefjord. This place is, on some sites, referred to more than hopefully as Oslo Sandefjord. Don't be fooled, this is an expensive hour and a half ride to the Norwegian capital. Norway is an expensive option anyway, so if you're going to go, you want to fly into somewhere with a bit of life. Sorry Sandefjord, but I have taken the prerogative of ditching you on David's behalf.

Instead I go back to the crop of Ryanair flights mysteriously hovering at £9.99. There are 20 in total, so I let Random.org make the choice on our behalf, and end up booking him a flight to Knock, a pilgrimage site in the west of Ireland, and the gateway to gorgeous County Mayo. Hopefully things should get easier from here on in. He flies out on Tuesday 23rd February at the very reasonable hour of 9.55 a.m.

After the three nights in Ireland, I need to find a Friday flight out on 26th February. So I start a new search on Skyscanner.

FROM:	Knock
TO:	Everywhere
DEPART:	*This time change to the* **specific day**, *then press* **Search**.

The cheapest flight is to Cologne, but when I click on it, it shows a 7.40 a.m. flight time, way before David's earliest start. I back-button to the search results and the second option is a flight to Frankfurt, the Manhattan of Germany, leaving at a far more respectable 12.30 p.m. The flight is listed as £14, but comes for just £12.99. Well thank you for your honesty, Ryanair. Time to search for our third destination leaving on Monday 29th February. Perhaps he will get proposed to on this flight!

FROM:	Frankfurt
TO:	Everywhere
DEPART:	Specific day, 29th February. Search. *Bish bash bosh!*

This is getting interesting. Having gone from rural Ireland to dynamic Frankfurt, I have two flights at £8, Milan and Venice. The

Venice flight is at 6.55 a.m. so it's Milan, the Italian fashion capital, leaving at 6.25 p.m., for a bargain £7.62.

FROM:	Milan
TO:	Everywhere
DEPART:	3rd March

There is a 6.15 a.m. flight to Bucharest, which sadly can't be taken. So the next cheapest option is a £9.72 flight back to Germany, to the cultural hub of Cologne.

FROM:	Cologne
TO:	Everywhere
DEPART:	6th March

This time the cheapest option is to lovely Copenhagen, Europe's new capital of cool. This one is a mere £7.62, with a 7.15 p.m. take-off time.

So time to find flight five, on Wednesday 9th March, and after this or the next one, according to Dave's brief, I have to start looking for flights back to London.

FROM:	Copenhagen
TO:	Everywhere
DEPART:	9th March

And here I find our cheapest flight so far, to dreamy, sexy Stockholm, for a mere £3.78, leaving at a most civilised 2.40 p.m. It's a weird anomaly but Scandinavian countries, despite being among the world's most expensive, have some of the most ridiculously cheap air ticket prices.

So flight six will either be home to London or, if the cost seems too high, according to Dave's brief, we can risk one more city, and hope for a cheap Tuesday flight back to The Smoke from wherever we find ourselves.

FROM:	Stockholm
TO:	Everywhere
DEPART:	12th March

The cheapest flight is back to Copenhagen for under £4 (these flights between the two Scandinavian capitals are good to note if you're looking for a cheap two-centre break). The next cheapest is to Warsaw for £7.32. There's a direct flight back to London for a mere £17, but I decide Warsaw is far too good and cheap to miss and I'll gamble on a reasonably priced flight back to London on the Tuesday. It's a 4 p.m. flight to Poland's buzzing capital, and a Saturday night out in Warsaw is not to be sniffed at.

So the next flight is our gamble return flight to London on the Tuesday. In reality, I would have already checked this out before I booked the flight to Warsaw, of course.

FROM:	Warsaw
TO:	London
DEPART:	15th March

And bingo! There are flights back to Stansted all day for £13.64. So there you have it, David's amazing three-week European jaunt is all booked. And here it is:

LONDON – KNOCK – FRANKFURT – MILAN – COLOGNE – COPENHAGEN – STOCKHOLM – WARSAW – LONDON

That's pretty cool, even if I do say so myself. All nice flights. And the cost, for eight flights?

TOTAL: £72.68

David, I think I have just surpassed myself…

SCENARIO TWO

MICHELLE: *I want a month-long adventure in the next few months, taking in the USA and maybe part of Latin America if it's affordable. I'm prepared to pay a little more to visit somewhere exotic. I don't mind staying over in some cool European cities before we go transatlantic. I want to fly from Manchester, but happy to come home via a London airport, where I can visit friends before returning up North. I have budgeted £600 for flights.*

OK, so let's start with a search from Manchester. Kiwi.com is adept at finding more convoluted transatlantic routes, but let's begin with Skyscanner. Again, make sure you have clicked on one-way. And unclick direct flights only.

FROM:	Manchester
TO:	United States
DEPART:	*Click on* **Whole Month** *and select* **Cheapest Month**

The first flight it finds me could be a tough one to beat, £200 on 9th May with good old Thomas Cook Airlines to Orlando. Orlando is often a great airport for heading into Latin America, but let's see what Kiwi.com can find for us. First of all I'm going to search for a flight from Manchester to the USA, but I'm also going to try it out for routes to Mexico and Colombia, two fabulous destinations with good low-cost airlines of their own.

FROM:	Manchester
TO:	United States
DEPART:	*Click on* **Date Range** *then I click my first date as* **Tomorrow,** **4th February,** *the last day*, **17th June.**
RETURN:	No Return

Now hit Search. OK, so already Kiwi.com has beaten Skyscanner by finding a route to New York for £159. The New York flight is via Dublin and Oslo on Tuesday 8th March, with Ryanair and then

Norwegian. Interesting. So if I'm going to take this deal, I'm going to factor in a bit of time in Ireland and Norway for Michelle before she crosses the pond. There is also an alternative route via Brussels and Copenhagen for £173, if that's more her bag. Or via Riga and Oslo for £175, with the Latvian capital offering superb value for money for a short stay; I'm very intrigued by this route, which seems to offer the best value break. So I'm aiming to nab that cheap Oslo–NYC flight on 8th March, leaving Manchester a few days earlier and spending a few nights in Riga and one or two in Oslo. But before we do that, let's look at Kiwi.com's options from Manchester to Mexico and Colombia. The cheapest Manchester–Mexico deal is at £255, with Kiwi.com finding a magical route flying first to Barcelona and then Verona, before disembarking in Cancun from a Meridiana flight. Now that deserves more exploration. There is also a route to Cancun via Oslo and Fort Lauderdale which could be a lot of fun. As I said earlier in this book, Kiwi.com's software is great for uncovering unusual routes, which you can then often nab for cheaper if you're staying in each location for a few days.

To Colombia, best price is an excellent £255, a lovely route through Copenhagen and Fort Lauderdale to gorgeous colonial gem Cartagena. I think this and the Verona–Cancun route are the most exciting. I may well look to see if I can follow these routes but for even less.

But I'm still intrigued by those Oslo and Copenhagen to New York fares. Including my European connections, I'm shaving around £100 off the fares to Cancun and Cartagena. If I can get these flights for even cheaper, £100 will take me a long way in my journey from the USA to Mexico or Colombia.

So I'm going to start by searching for the cheapest fares between Norway and the USA and Denmark and the USA, then work backwards from there. The transatlantic elements of my trip are always going to be the most expensive, so it's best to get these as cheaply as possible, then work around them, to plan my itinerary.

So back to Kiwi.com…

FROM:	Norway
TO:	United States
DEPART:	Up to six months from today

Remember, no return. Then Search. OK, from Norway, the cheapest flight is direct from Oslo to Fort Lauderdale on the afternoon of Wednesday 9th March for £123.80. That means we've still got £32 to spend getting to Oslo, compared with the cheapest flight we found earlier. That's a lot of spondooliks in European airfare terms. Let's quickly repeat the same search with Denmark instead of Norway. The cheapest this time is £140. Not bad, but I'm going to grab that Oslo/Fort Lauderdale nugget. The Florida town is a nice place for a few days, and I know there are some great connections to Latin America.

So now we need to get from Manchester to Oslo to catch our flight on 9th March. I'm going to allow for up to a week for Michelle to meander her way to Florida from Europe. So back on Kiwi.com, this is what I do.

FROM:	Manchester
TO:	Oslo
DEPART:	*Click on* **Date Range** *and highlight the* **seven days before**
	9th March. *(Beware! Kiwi.com also does a 'quality' search,*
	where it lists its results according to some spurious
	measurements. Always, always, make sure your results are
	sorted by price to get the best deals.)

So the cheapest route to Oslo leaves exactly a week before you depart for America, costs £22.16 and is direct. We don't want to bankrupt Michelle by leaving her for a week in Oslo, so we are looking for non-direct connections. The fourth one down the list fits the bill, listed as taking 24 hours and costing £28.28. There are tons of these babies, as it happens, all going via God's own city Dublin. So my route is clear. I'm going to aim for two nights in one of these cities and one in another. Which means I need a decent flight to Dublin on 6th March... Now I'm switching back to Skyscanner, because the actual flights tend to be cheaper (they don't charge a commission; though usually I book half my flights with Kiwi.com as they open up a world of options for me and I'm happy to pay the small commission as a tip).

FROM:	Manchester
TO:	Dublin
DEPART:	*Click* **Specific date** *then* **6th March Search...**

The cheapest is the £9.99 flight, leaving at 8 a.m., which leaves a full day for breakfast and Sunday lunch in the Irish capital. Booked. Next:

FROM:	Dublin
TO:	Oslo
DEPART:	*Click* Date Range *then pick* 8th–9th March

Oddly, the price the next day, from Dublin to Oslo, is the same as the price from London to Oslo via Dublin. I still reckon it's worth shelling out the extra £10 and having a night on the craic than heading straight to Oslo, but of course that's your call. I book my flight through Skyscanner and save a little cash. Tuesday is showing flights for £15.31, which is a lot cheaper than the Kiwi. com deal. So that's another flight booked and Michelle still has almost a full day to explore the beautiful Norwegian capital before she heads to Fort Lauderdale.

So to recap, here is her itinerary so far...

Sunday 6th March	Manchester to Dublin	£9.99
Tuesday 8th March	Dublin to Oslo	£15.31
Wednesday 9th March	Oslo to Fort Lauderdale	£123.80
	RUNNING TOTAL	**£149.10**

Which is a tenner cheaper than anything I found on my original search, and we've got stays in two more countries. Nice work!

Next, before we go off roaming all around the Americas, I'm going to look ahead to my transatlantic flight home. If I get that booked now, I'll know how much we have to play with across the pond. Michelle began her holiday on 6th March, and she wants to be away for a month, so I'm looking at transatlantic flights between 27th March and 4th April, which will give her time to mosey back slowly and maybe make some more stopovers before she lands in either Manchester or London. So I'm going to do three Kiwi.com searches for those dates from USA, Mexico and Colombia to the United Kingdom. I might throw in some searches from the latter two to Spain also, because I know there are good connections for historical reasons, and it's easy to get a cheap flight from Madrid or Barcelona back home.

FROM:	United States
TO:	United Kingdom
DEPART:	*Click* Date Range *then pick from* 27th March–4th April

On the USA search, there is a direct flight from New York to London for £177. I check the flights via Norway and Oslo, but London really is the cheapest option. I throw in a few other countries and Ponta Delgada in the gorgeous Portuguese Azores comes up for £144.43 from Boston, on Saturday 2nd April. Now that would be a spectacular place to end her jaunt, and it's £33 cheaper than the flight direct to London, so if I can find a flight from the Azores to London or Manchester for around that figure, she would be effectively enjoying the Azores sublime subtropical beauty for free. That sounds like my kind of holiday!

I do my Mexico search and the best is a direct flight from Cancun to Manchester for £238. But direct schmirect. Michelle wants an adventure. And Colombia turns out to be way too expensive.

So *let's do that Boston/Azores flight!* Michelle would land in the Azores early on Sunday 3rd April; assuming she would want at least two days there, how much would it cost to get her home? Let's stay with Kiwi.com.

FROM:	Ponta Delgada
TO:	United Kingdom
DEPART:	4th April–7th April

There's a route via Lisbon, leaving early morning on the Wednesday 6th for £60. Now Lisbon would be another great stopover. So let's see what we can find booking the flights independently.

FROM:	Ponta Delgada
TO:	Portugal
DEPART:	4th April–7th April

That's a lot more like it, there's an early morning flight from the Azores to Lisbon on the Tuesday 5th April, for £17.58. Can we get home for less than the £43 price difference, with a night or more in the Portuguese capital...?

FROM:	Lisbon
TO:	United Kingdom
DEPART:	6th–9th April

And what do we find: £40 to Manchester, leaving at 10 a.m. on Friday 8th April, changing at... guess? Dublin with Ryanair. There's a seven hour layover in Dublin, or she can fly just to Dublin direct for £31.33 and catch a flight to Manchester the following day for £9.17, which I will book her in for. Phew! So there we now also have the return leg of her trip....

Saturday 2nd April	Boston to Ponta Delgada	£144
Tuesday 5th April	Ponta Delgada to Lisbon	£17
Friday 8th April	Lisbon to Dublin	£31
Saturday 9th April	Dublin to Manchester	£9
	TOTAL FOR RETURN LEG:	£201
	RUNNING TOTAL:	**£350.10**

So that's Michelle's transatlantic trip sorted; now we only have to fill in the gaps between Fort Lauderdale on 9th March and Boston on 2nd April, taking in some Latin spirit. This is the fun bit! Boston is a big hub city, with connections from lots of places, so it shouldn't be difficult to find our way back there. Let's start by searching where to head to first. I reckon Fort Lauderdale's laid back beach life could entertain her for anything from four nights to a week, and she needs time to relax after hurrying through Dublin and Oslo. So let's go to Kiwi.com. and see where the flights out of town are.

FROM:	Fort Lauderdale
TO:	Anywhere
DEPART:	13th–17th March

Cheapest out of the blocks is Baltimore at a mere £28. Then under £40 are Atlanta, Tampa, Cleveland, Orlando, San Antonio, Niagara Falls, Indianapolis, Greenville and Knoxville. Incredibly, the Bahamas are a mere £47, the Turks and Caicos Islands 48, and I know they could stir Michelle's love for the exotic, perhaps a little more than Ohio. I have a better idea. It's a toss-up between Mexico City and Colombia's magical capital Bogota, but I'm going to try to get there, in the hope we can catch a cheap flight and indulge our Caribbean fantasies in Cartagena afterwards, and who knows, we might yet reach Mexico. I know this because I've been playing with these search engines for longer than is healthy... So once you're in Fort Lauderdale, Colombia and Mexico come cheap. And there we have it, Kiwi.com has a 10.25 a.m. flight to Bogota, with the excellent Spirit Airlines, on Monday 14th March for £56. When I go to the booking site, the flight is actually on sale for $64. That's £44! Result. OK, let's now try and get that flight to Cartagena for some Caribbean magic. I'm giving Michelle a minimum of three nights in Bogota, and stick with Kiwi.com.

FROM:	Bogota
TO:	Anywhere
DEPART:	7th–20th March

Cartagena turns out to be a mere £28 from Bogota, leaving in the afternoon of Thursday 17th March in time for a weekend of Caribbean colonial revelry. Result.

Skyscanner's month-long search comes into its own here, and it shows me that there's a £96 flight with Spirit Airlines back to Fort Lauderdale on the afternoon of Wednesday 23rd. Booked and sorted. That gives us around ten days to get back up to Boston. This time we won't linger too long in Fort Lauderdale.

FROM:	Fort Lauderdale
TO:	Anywhere
DEPART:	24th–26th March

Now I need to get back to Boston. Using Kiwi.com again, our options are many for around the £30 mark. Baltimore is the cheapest, a city of which I know nothing. I fancy San Antonio for £34, but it's a 7 a.m. flight. Boston is only £40, but she's not going to spend *that* much time there. But Atlanta, Georgia, is a cool city I can fly to on the 24th, nice afternoon flight, £41. Booked and done. Atlanta deserves at least three nights, so I'm looking to leave after a minimum four nights.

So, I think one more city before Boston. And we definitely need a minimum of two nights in the New England beauty. So, let's try via Kiwi.com, first of all asking for a route to Boston. I don't want to go there directly, but Kiwi.com will be able to show me the cheapest route stopping off somewhere else and maybe inspire me on some imaginative combinations.

FROM:	Atlanta
TO:	Anywhere
DEPART:	28th–31st March

The cheapest flights which are not direct are around the £75 mark and they are via either Chicago or Philadelphia. So I'm going to search again for a single to each. I'd seriously be happy to break the journey with either. Chicago, is of course, one of the USA's most iconic citadels, while Philadelphia bows to no man, having once been the second city of the British Empire.

So I repeat the above search, replacing Atlanta with Chicago and then Philadelphia.

There are cheap flights to Chicago for £28, but 6.30 a.m. flights are a non-starter. The best decently timed flight is on Tuesday 29th March at around 10 a.m. for £42. Pretty decent, but let's see what Philadelphia has got to offer. There's a good flight on Wednesday 30th March into Philly, but it's a late night one and doesn't give her much time there. I'm going to bagsy that flight from Atlanta to Chicago, then, on 29th March, which ideally will give her two or three nights in both glamorous Chicago and Boston, for £42. So my last flight needs to leave Chicago on either 31st March or 1st April to Boston. I'll get the cheapest flight leaving at a decent hour. So…

FROM:	Chicago
TO:	Boston
DEPART:	31st March–1st April

The best deal I can find is on Friday 1st April from Chicago to Boston, early afternoon, for £63. This gives me a very civilised three nights in Chicago and two in Boston before the beautiful journey home. Snapped up.

So now we have Michelle's complete 34-day itinerary, taking in 10 different cities, three continents and five different countries:

MANCHESTER – DUBLIN – OSLO – FORT LAUDERDALE – BOGOTA – CARTAGENA – FORT LAUDERDALE – ATLANTA – CHICAGO – BOSTON – PONTA DELGADA – LISBON – DUBLIN – MANCHESTER

TOTAL: £664

for Europe, America, Colombia, the Caribbean and the Azores

To put that in context, the cheapest direct return flights from Manchester to Chicago, with British Airways and American Airlines, travelling in and out on the same dates as above come in at £523. For £130 extra, you get an extra continent, and nine more cities.

I'd call that the trip of a lifetime, but it is by no means the cheapest or the best you could come up with. But hopefully by reading through the methods employed, you have worked out how to find your own bargain itineraries, dreamed a little bit, and found some interesting connections. Any trip that links Chicago, Colombia and the Azores gets my thumbs up, that's for sure.

CHAPTER 11

THE LAST RESORT

Like all true eccentrics, Oslo has absolutely no concept of how cuckoo it really is. It sits back in its raffia rocking chair, strokes its non-hipster beard, observes the world with a bemused squint and then calmly reassures itself it is completely sane and it is the rest of the world which is mad.

Oslo, I have to admit, had never really been high on my 'must visit' list. I'd been to Copenhagen and thoroughly enjoyed it; and to Helsinki, which is to Scandinavia what Croydon is to London, kind of a Poundland version of a Nordic paradise, Poundinavia. Like someone was given the basic concept of Scandinavia – clean air, nice stuff, good furniture, meatballs and jam, Russian threat, tall beautiful people – and then given ten minutes to create it. I'd passed through Stockholm en route to a Swedish baronial castle to interview Agnetha from ABBA in the midst of a winter blizzard, which seemed to me to be a pretty much utopian Scandinavian experience and very possibly my last trip to this part of the world as it was hard to imagine how it could ever be bettered.

So Oslo was an unexpected last stop; especially as I'd been told an orange juice would cost £98.55, and it was cold as hell freezing over. But the flight was incredibly cheap from Poland and I knew there were also stupidly inexpensive fares back to London. Anyway I'd spent next to nothing in Poland. Also it meant I'd now visited the whole Scandinavian big four, like getting all the stations in Monopoly, and it would therefore afford me the opportunity to rattle on about Scandinavia as if I know what I'm talking about, as I am no doubt about to do – too good a chance to turn that down.

I arrived late in the evening. Most of my flights in the first half of my trip tended to be morning affairs, while latterly they had been evening. It's certainly more civilised to travel later in the day, but arriving by night can be disorienting. Not seeing the landscape can alienate you from a place. I jump on a clean coach for the hour-long journey into town (Ryanair's Rygge base is a way out of the city centre). I drive through black before being delivered at a concrete lump redolent of a super-clean, super-charmless motorway service station. My phone has died, so I have absolutely no idea where I am in proximity to my hotel or the city centre. After stumbling about feeling very lost for a while I am directed by a pizza salesman to an awful, thudding, unreconstructed heavy metal bar fall of porky, unglamorous Scandos bashing their fists and banging their heads to music so lacking in any kind of subtlety, nuance or finesse it would even be rejected in the County Durham countryside. I order a drink and ask the barman to charge my phone behind the bar. In Poland I would have just leapt in a cab, but I daren't risk it here. I was rich in Poland and I'm poor in Norway. Money buys freedom. Already I feel less free in Norway. After 20 minutes I ask for my phone back.

It's still as dead as Sinatra. He forgot to turn on the switch. I settle down for another 20 minutes of head thumping in a bar that makes the pubs of Reading Station feel like they belong on the Champs Élysées. So far the experience is definitely more Finland than Sweden.

I finally get my phone online to locate my hotel's address and ask a drunk oil executive banging his head next to me how much it's likely to set me back in a taxi. Under 20 euros, he advises, and I gratefully leap into a cab.

We twist and turn a few blocks and I'm at my hotel, the Skandic Vulcan. There is a raucous party going on outside, and numerous exceedingly drunk people milling about. I remember it's a Saturday night. I hop up to my room, which is extraordinary. The Skandic Vulcan is like a Travelodge done by Damien Hirst. Offering only the basics, no pool, no restaurant, no mini bar, small rooms, it is nevertheless designed impeccably and festooned with art. My door is encased in work by a local artist, as is my room.

'We have a little present for you,' says the girl on reception, which turns out to be the art festooned all over my room. The hotel is bright and beautiful and affordable.

I'm impressed but still disoriented. I leave my room and hear a woman crying plaintively from a not quite closed bedroom door, 'Help! Help!'

I push the door open and she falls over the corner of the bed.

'Oh thank God! No light switch,' she says. I pop her keycard into the slot and she is bathed in light, and bleary eyed. I leave and then get stuck in the service lift for five minutes, entirely through my own stupidity. Yes, definitely time to call it quits for the night.

There is no restaurant here but they do have a fridge full of butties and I bag myself a ham and cheese baguette and retire in my very comfy bed ready to start afresh with Oslo tomorrow, utterly confused as to what sort of place I have landed myself in.

The next morning I awake to bright sunshine and a text from Mariel, a new American friend who I had met on the flight on the way over, who was checking into the hotel this lunchtime after spending her first night with her aunt out in the countryside. We've missed breakfast, but I order cake, coffee and a glass of French white wine for her while she waits for her room to become available. I'm already nervous about the cost but I needn't have worried. The girl on the bar stiffens as I order the drink, a response I notice a few times in Oslo. Norwegians stiffen quickly when faced with things they don't comprehend.

'You can't have that,' she says sharply as I make my order.

'Eh?'

'A drink! You can't have a drink. I can't serve you wine.'

'Really? Why?'

She looks flustered, a bit pissed off with me, and embarrassed. 'It's Sunday. You cannot have an alcoholic drink in Norway before 2 p.m. on a Sunday,' she snaps.

'No? Why? That's ridiculous.' It's already 1 p.m. and half of Newcastle will be paralytic by now. Meanwhile poor Mariel is looking shamefaced, and I suggest she attend the next local AA meeting.

The waitress gives me a wry glance and I can't tell if she's joking or not when she shrugs. 'Because you're in Norway now. Get used to it.'

It's not strictly true. You can imbibe booze in Norway before 2 p.m. on a Sunday, I think, but only if you drink it privately in your home. I'm not sure how the law applies should we have drunk it in our hotel bedroom, for instance. Well, you see, there are a lot of laws in Norway. So while I think it may be legal to do that, we could not pop out now and buy it from a shop or supermarket. We would have had to have bought it a day earlier, from a special government-licenced alcohol store, a *vinmonopolet*, which are only permitted to open until 3 p.m. on Saturday or 6 p.m. midweek. Even when you *are* permitted to buy alcohol in a bar, don't go looking for lethal cocktails, or large doubles. Norwegians are only allowed to imbibe liquor shots containing up to 6cl of alcohol. Then again you could, in theory, buy two single shots and pour them into the same glass. But I'm not sure whether the act of putting them into one glass constitutes a crime or not. All of this makes last night's roaring drunk Saturday night Oslo crowd all the more confusing. This isn't Prohibition, but the Norwegian state has assembled such a prissy, pissy, meddling attitude towards libations that surely causes more not less consumption.

Everyone knows people who are forced to drink at home get more inebriated. I recently met a Frenchman who recoiled in horror when I told him I was from Newcastle. He recalled walking from the station to his hotel and past a Dantean vision of drunkenness including grown men being sick over their kebabs and young ladies crawling on all fours with their skirts tucked in their knickers over glass-strewn cobblestones streaked with hot streams of piss.

'Ah, that'll be the Bigg Market,' I told him.

Newcastle's insane levels of inebriation, I believe, date back from the years, which I can still remember, when the last drop drunk in a pub had to be imbibed by 10.45 p.m., 15 minutes before anywhere else in the country. Britain then, like Norway now, was addicted to telling people what to do and how to do it. Then enforcing it in law. Consequently the Geordie nation would dive out of the office and factory at 5.30 p.m. and by 6.30 p.m. would have downed three treble malibus and two pints of Skol. The relaxation of the licensing laws allowed people to drink at a more leisurely pace, but by then it was too late; gulping down booze furiously while nervously watching the clock tick became embedded in the Geordie DNA. After sitting with my ashamed-looking American friend, who I think just went back to her room for a little cry, I set out to explore my sixth capital city of the trip (I'm including Barcelona, because, well, it is).

But is this? Granted, I'm used to London, but I wander through the city outskirts past a closed 'convenience' store, closed restaurant, closed bar, closed pub and lots of closed Thai massage parlours. *Lots* of closed massage parlours. I'm guessing the preponderance of such establishments is somehow linked to the oil industry, but perhaps that's unfair. Either way the purchase of sex is illegal in Norway, even if the selling of it is not. I've seen livelier Sundays in Colwyn Bay in January, quite frankly. I pass a concert hall advertising a performance by Leonard Cohen, and then I see an advertisement for an exhibition by Oslo's most famous son Edvard Munch, and finally I kinda understand the state of mind which inspired *The Scream*. I had hoped my trip would end with a bang but I worry, during my three nights here, if it's going to deflate like a wrinkled, forgotten party balloon. A few more twists and turns, though, and I'm in a livelier street. There's a bar showing English top-flight football, though it's Sunderland vs Newcastle so there's nothing top quality about it. Nevertheless, it's a relief. People are drinking beer and being normal, and though it's a bit of a faceless chain, I'm glad of the atmosphere. *Any* kind of atmosphere. Remarkably, a good quarter of the punters are wearing black and white Newcastle shirts. At first I think the Toon Army fans are expats, the sing-song Oslo accent from a distance sounding uncannily like Geordie in rhythm, pitch and guttural lilt. As their drinking exploits prove, Geordies are the sons and daughters of Vikings, and when a Geordie talks about 'gannin' hjem', the word hjem (home) derives directly from Old Norse. But Norwegians have long taken to the Toon, since Munch's *The Scream* became our most high-profile foreign supporter. Previously a happy-go-lucky chap known for his love of practical jokes and tomfoolery, over years and years of trekking to Saint James Park to see his favourite team humiliated at home by Watford or whoever, he morphed into the man we see on the paintings before us today. Poor bugger. After sucking clean eight teriyaki chicken wings (I know, but I am craving non-European flavours after a month away) and watching Newcastle lose inevitably to their most bitter rivals, and seeing how Norwegian Magpies' fans faithfully recreate the Geordie tradition of handwringing and head slapping, I step out into an unrecognisable Oslo. The streets are busy, the fountains are fizzy, the warmth is almost Mediterranean, and the daylight is dazzling. The mid-afternoon autumn light is a gorgeous melange of golds which makes the city look as if it has been touched by King Midas. I walk down to the bay, where the golds are joined by shards of silver and the light is almost blinding. Oslo, for the first time, looks really beautiful and I stop internally muttering. Yes, it's expensive and yes it's a little officious. It's no use comparing it to London, or to its Danish cousin Copenhagen, where nobody pays any attention whatsoever to rules. This is Oslo. A little *Twin Peaks*. A little Bree van der Kampe. A little Roy Cropper. But utterly captivating if you just give in to it.

The afternoon is short in Oslo in October, however, and soon I'm looking for some nightlife.

The straight scene seems to be mainly football chain pubs, restaurants, heavy metal bars and really lairy karaoke places. So I use an app on my phone called Grindr which gives you a menu of the nearest online available gentlemen, arranged as a grid. Useful if it's a hottie in the next door hotel room, problematic if it's your straight, married boss. It's also useful for locating some good nightlife. To be honest, it's more useful as a tool for finding out local information, when abroad, than tracking down sexual malarkey. It's just something to put on, to direct your feet when you are faced with a myriad of choices. It's like spinning the roulette wheel of life. I like spinning the roulette wheel of life. It really isn't about sex. It just tends to make me go... ooh, okay then, I'll go there. When I'm in Selfridges' food court I feel paralysed with choice. I guess being in a strange city can feel the same, but I turn this on, and I'm kind of just taken off on a journey not of my own making.

I'd visited Ett Glass – a chunky, earthily glamorous little bar, all dark wood and cosy corners, serving amazing riffs on every kind of salmon you can imagine – during the day time without clocking that it is a mixed gay bar. Norwegian gay men are pretty much identical to Norwegian straight men: healthy, handsome, built like they chop down trees with their forearms, about eight foot tall. Actually they might be really camp but I just couldn't really pick up on much they were saying, being a far shorter 5'11", stood back straight with my hair blow-dried. On my night-time visit, there seem to be no gay men present, just a few girls gossiping and three handsome, outdoorsy, eight foot fishermen/lumberjack types chatting over a jug of beer. Probably discussing some reindeer they shot, or wolf they shooed off or something or other. I observe how much more relaxed Norwegian straight men are with each other, huddled closer to each other, not afraid to pat each other's shoulders, or squeeze each other's arms. Ruffling each other's hair. What a breath of fresh air. Scandinavia really is ahead of the curve.

'So what do you think of the Oslo gay scene?' the one with the Morton Harket dimples in the middle asks me in a manful fashion. Wow! These Scandinavians are so cool and unfazed by homosexuality, I think, smiling.

'It's my first foray,' I say, nonchalantly.

'Well, welcome,' says the middle one. 'I'm Nils, this is my new boyfriend Pieter and this is my best friend Markus.'

My 15-year-old self does a backflip.

The three lumberjacks, who actually work in media, architecture and design, somehow without being snotty toe-rags (go figure – another Norwegian eccentricity, I guess) take me to the real epicentre of the Oslo gay scene, the London pub. This is a red hued subterranean place with lots of little booths where people huddle around whispering and gossiping about the people in the booth to the left of them, a karaoke space and dance area, bars that people sit at and flirt and make merry around, and a clientele which collectively barely glances at its smartphone. It's ironic that it is named after London because you'd never find anywhere this convivial in Soho these days, gay or straight; it would have been turned into flats or Pret a Manger or something else we don't have nearly enough of already.

I'm a fan of anywhere subterranean and windowless since my days hanging out in Corbieres wine bar in the Halcyon days of Smiths/ New Order/Stone Roses Manchester. They're the bits nobody else wants, and consequently filled with the best people ever. All the pretentious wankers who want to see and be seen (I think that was an Eighties concept) steer clear, leaving the basement bars to the people you'd actually want to knock about with. Nils and Pieter meander off at some point and, just to be neighbourly, I pop out to visit Markus's house in the Oslo suburbs. It's a wooden structure, slightly dilapidated in a perfect kind of way, stylishly dishevelled inside. Damn these Scandinavians with their stylish dishevelment. My flat just looks like a student or Tracey Emin has been squatting there, in every possible sense. We park at the bottom of a very large incline and I climb a hill, then once into his flat, some stairs and then pine ladders and smoke a joint in a loft. It's all almost too perfect, like something from a film. There are things just thrown around, like someone just dumped them there nonchalantly, and yet it really does seem like someone came in and manicured every bit of imperfection. If Kurt Cobain was an apartment, he would look like this.

The next morning, Markus tells me to 'use the blue towel'. I'm a little floaty and happy to have immersed myself so effortlessly in local life and mistakenly pick up the red towel. As he is bidding me farewell, Markus looks hurt and somewhat displeased.

'Thank you for your visit,' he tells me. 'May I ask you something?'

Errm yes..?

'Why did you use the red towel when I asked you to use the blue one…?'

Oslo can afford to be perfectionist. Literally. This country is stinking rich. Ruled by Danes, then Swedes, who always looked down their noses at their Norwegian country cousins, Oslo was church-mouse poor. Copenhagen and Stockholm were the glittering northern jewels and nobody much bothered with Christiania, as it used to be known. Even in World War II, Nazi-occupied Norway was a relative backwater. Ten thousand Norwegians died in the war, which is horrific in any other terms other than World War II. When Norway struck black gold in 1969, it was a chance to raise a solitary middle finger to those who had belittled or overlooked Oslo. The Norwegians, of course, being Norwegian, chose to underreact to their newfound fortune and the city is a model of stoic northern restraint. Oslo's hulking Opera House, for instance, manages to be both gargantuan and almost invisible to the human eye. It blends seamlessly and reflectively with the pristine Norwegian setting. I sit there over lunch, drinking the appliest apple juice you will ever taste, watching the river sparkle in silver and gold, and eating roast cod followed by beef cheeks. The cod is as pure as a Norwegian conscience. Simple and unadulterated with spice or tang. It's been a long arduous month of excellent, simple, classic European food. God that cod would be good rogan josh'd.

I walk into the pristine city centre, with its pristine people, and I've got to say I'm charmed. Whatever the opposite of higgledy-piggledy is, that's Oslo. I did see a hippy commune at the beginning of my stay, but even that was incredibly tidy and ordered. Yes, it's a bit Stepford, but it's eccentric more than annoyingly anal. I once went to the Florida Keys, which is obsessed with labelling everywhere as paradise, when it's clearly actually a big motorway with bits of islands stuck to the sides. I saw one man-made beach, Paradise Cove or Lagoon or something, where the sand is literally combed every single day and the palm trees grow exactly five metres apart. I lay on my paradise sun lounger and couldn't escape the feeling of anxiety. If Hitler did beaches, they'd look like this. Norway isn't like this. True, everybody without exception is gorgeous. There are no old people, because the folk in their seventies look about 35, tingling with health thanks to clean air, natural food, clear consciences that come from living in utopia and eating cod which comes sans sauce.

Everybody dresses exactly the same as everyone else, and they all look fab in their urban casuals like a great big Gap advert. The men are about eight foot tall in their mohair socks, the women are pretty, giggly, sparkly and also tall. It's really, really, really nice so long as you don't step out of line. I *like* Oslo and I want to go back, if, for nothing else, to sleep with some of the most perfect people on the planet, who seem to have a thing for tired, middle aged, greying dwarfs. My dating app is in meltdown. Little wonder. I *am* the counterculture.

Monday night is livelier than Sunday, but it's still quiet compared to every other city I've visited on my trip. Right now I like it that way. I go back to one of the places from last night for a bit of food. The barman is even shorter than me. And he's Norwegian. Which can't be easy. He's looking rattled and at one point he shoots out from behind the counter and chases someone up the road like a mad banshee. I'd seen the fur throws, lovingly laid on the patio chairs on the main street outside the bar. The barman comes back fuming, clutching one. Apparently some drunk student girl helped herself to one as she walked past and mine host gave chase. He's puce with fury when he returns, so I expect she got a bit of a shock. 'I grabbed her and said, 'What are you doing, you retard?' he says proudly. 'She screamed, "Hey, get off me, you gay!" And I'm not even a gay!' He tells me, exasperated.

'Mate, I'm losing count of the hate crimes occurring here,' I laugh, trying to lighten the mood. He's now incandescent, tapping his head. 'What's wrong with these people?' He's genuinely upset.

'Let me give you a hand bringing in the throws. They'd all disappear within five minutes in Britain,' I tell him, hoping that will assuage his fears over the mad criminality in Norway.

He stares at me like I am mad. 'No! This is Norway, not Britain. We don't behave like that here. I want the throws out there. I want them to be warm and inviting for our customers.'

I feel bad for him. I really do. This is a very Scandinavian crime. I come across this attitude time and time again, sheer exasperation. Not at the fact that someone *did* break the rules. But that they *could*. To even contemplate it is to invite Norwegian apoplexy. What a funny place. They're really kind and naturally soft, yet incredibly uptight. It's like a parallel universe Britain. Our nearest cousins in many ways. Britain Through the Looking Glass. How people always wanted Britain to be, y'know. Bowler hats, BBC English, Fanny Craddock... Then Johnny Rotten and Princess Di came along and fucked it all up. Right now I'm ready to have my lovely, imperfect, fat, short, non-utopian UK back. But bless that poor distraught lad, and bless Norway for even being bothered to attempt perfection.

I think we gave up after Diana died. Just collectively decided, as she did, that perfection was a rotten burden to place on anyone. And then, thank god, embraced the imperfect. I love my home!

The air is nice tonight as I walk around town. No wind. Just crisp cold. Clean cold. Warm cold. Back at the London pub, Markus is there with an equally handsome, statuesque bloke. We chat and dance. I order a couple of orange juices to take back to my room, as the hotel bar will be closed and there's no fridge to raid.

'You *can't* take that home with you!' says the barmaid in shock when I suggest such a thing.

'What? Why?' I ask.

'Because it's against the *rules*,' she says in pure horror.

'Whose rules?'

She shakes her head and walks out the back.

'That's crazy,' I say, slipping them into my bag.

'You can't do *that*,' says the horrified bloke sitting on my left.

'Why?'

'Because it's against the *rules*.'

'In London we just ignore daft rules,' I tell him. 'The police don't even bother.'

The man stares at me wide-eyed. 'You will be a criminal!'

Norway loves laws and rules order. It's beautiful and lovable because you don't ever feel like it comes from a mean, superior or controlling place. But you could not, *I* could not fall in love with somewhere so uptight. Markus and his friend Jakub come back to my room for a nightcap. As they leave, I notice for the first time the picture of Marlene Dietrich glaring at me.

'And I suppose *you* never did, right?' I scowl back at her.

The next morning I wait to catch the bus from the hotel to Oslo Central station, determined to avoid a Brussels type situation which would bankrupt me here in Scandinavia. When it arrives, it's tiny. Seven people in front of me clamber on board and the driver holds up his hand to say no more. Oh fuck, here we go again.

'Please! I will miss my flight,' I beg the driver. He shakes his head. 'It's against the rules.'

I give him full-force puppy dog eyes. And he reluctantly relents. Maybe he's an Italian, deep down. Phew, whatever the weather, I made it. The driver looks devastated as he drives me. No, he's definitely Norwegian. At the station I'm still running late and scrambling around for my train. I go to the help desk. Unlike in Brussels or Barcelona or Rome or, my goodness, anywhere in Britain ,there are about 20 people in red jackets proffering me assistance. I make my train with plenty of time to spare as a young lass walks me to my embarkation point. I heart you Oslo, I really do you know. You were far from being my last resort.

The train takes me on the most scenic, most beautiful journey so far past ordered houses and ordered lives, beautiful modernist breeze block suburban homes that would look like shit if they were back in Britain. The sun is blazing. In the autumn light I pass landscapes drizzled in honey which are almost certainly the most beautiful I have ever cast my eyes upon. Beautiful, perfect, perfectly imperfect Norway. There'll be nothing this nice travelling back from Essex I reckon.

But you know, it's not delirium: the autumn sun is out and even the countryside south of Stansted looks beautiful today.

Isn't it odd that we now take for granted that one moment we can be in one place and the next somewhere a thousand miles and a thousand cities, cultures and experiences away? For less than the price of a pie, for goodness sake. But today, after being away so long, and actually forgetting what home feels like, it does feel really weird to be back here. And for all my mad experiences I do know that I live in the maddest place of all. My lovely home. London, where on a daily basis I get a little taste of everything I have experienced on my jaunt around the continent. I was going to try to say something clever, but I've nothing really, to add, other than, it's good to be back. What an incredible adventure. Sorry to harp on. But £144? Get outta here! Ooh I love travel. Ooh I love coming home.